FEEDING THE NATION IN WORLD WAR II

For my Parents

FEEDING
THE
NATION
IN WORLD WAR II
Rationing, Digging for Victory and Unusual Food

Craig Armstrong

PEN & SWORD
HISTORY

AN IMPRINT OF PEN & SWORD BOOKS LTD.
YORKSHIRE – PHILADELPHIA

First published in Great Britain in 2022 by
PEN AND SWORD HISTORY
An imprint of
Pen & Sword Books Ltd
Yorkshire – Philadelphia

ISBN 978 1 52672 517 2

A CIP catalogue record for this book is available from the British Library.

Typeset in Times New Roman 12/16 by
SJmagic DESIGN SERVICES, India.
Printed and bound in the UK by CPI Group (UK) Ltd.

Pen & Sword Books Limited incorporates the imprints of Atlas, Archaeology,
Aviation, Discovery, Family History, Fiction, History, Maritime, Military,
Military Classics, Politics, Select, Transport, True Crime, Air World, Frontline
Publishing, Leo Cooper, Remember When, Seaforth Publishing, The Praetorian
Press, Wharncliffe Local History, Wharncliffe Transport, Wharncliffe True Crime
and White Owl.

For a complete list of Pen & Sword titles please contact
PEN & SWORD BOOKS LIMITED
47 Church Street, Barnsley, South Yorkshire, S70 2AS, England
E-mail: enquiries@pen-and-sword.co.uk
Website: www.pen-and-sword.co.uk

Or

PEN AND SWORD BOOKS
1950 Lawrence Rd, Havertown, PA 19083, USA
E-mail: Uspen-and-sword@casematepublishers.com
Website: www.penandswordbooks.com

Contents

Introduction

A common view of the countryside during the war holds that rural areas had it better than urban. There was less bombing, more and a greater variety of food available and a more relaxed lifestyle. This view can be challenged. It was clear from the outset that any future war with Germany would have a huge effect on the British countryside. The immediate post-war intentions of protectionism, subsidies and price controls for British agriculture were intended to enable Britain to be less dependent upon food imports (a situation which had almost seen Britain starved out of the First World War) had been destroyed by the economic depression of the 1920s and 1930s which had badly disrupted British farming and had seen the country continue to import vast quantities of foodstuffs.

Britain had slipped back into the bad habit of becoming hugely reliant on imported food and this dependence upon imported food was a massive weakness if Britain was to be involved in another war. The government established that the country imported approximately 70 per cent of its food and that this required some 20 million tons of shipping every year. Imports of butter were a huge 91 per cent, along with 80 per cent of fruits, 70 per cent of cheese and sugar, 70 per cent of cereals and fats, and 50 per cent of meat. The imports came from a wide variety of countries but the Empire and the Dominions were a major source. New Zealand alone covered 50 per cent of the cheese imports, 25 per cent of butter, and 17 per cent of meat (mainly lamb).

The expected future war would thus place a huge burden upon British farming (which had become almost moribund in places) to produce more food, while at the same time radical measures such as rationing would have to be immediately introduced. In addition, the countryside had far more problems than those which could be found in farming.

Although the government had been planning, in a fitful manner, for food production issues in the event of a war since the early 1930s, this planning had suffered inertia largely due to the hope that was placed upon the policy of appeasement favoured by Neville Chamberlain when he became Prime Minister in 1937.

Nevertheless, it had been recognised that rationing would be an inevitable part of any such scheme and, despite severe misgivings and a lack of enthusiasm amongst many in government, initial planning did take place. Rationing had to be planned well in advance due to the sheer difficulties of such a massive countrywide scheme. Despite this recognition, it was agreed that rationing would not be applied immediately upon the outbreak of war but would only be imposed once there were prolonged shortages or shortages of critical foodstuffs.

The administrative demands were immense. Firstly, it was envisaged that details of every man, woman and child would have to be filled out in a household form. This form was to include sections where individual retailers were nominated by the householder. These included a baker's for bread, a butcher's shop for meat, etc. These forms would then be used to draw up ration books which would be issued to each person. To ensure against fraud, the issuance of ration books had to be tied to a national registration scheme and accompanying national registration certificate. Ration books would last for six months and would include separate coupons for each rationed item of food and there would be separate books for adults, adolescent boys, expectant mothers, children under the age of six. Those involved in heavy work, those whose work involved extensive travel, and soldiers and other service personnel on leave were also issued with separate ration books. Other categories were added later but this was obviously a hugely complicated and ponderous scheme which required a great deal of manpower to manage and administrate.

Another added level of administrative complexity involved the retailers, each of whom would be allocated a permit enabling them to purchase an amount of food commensurate with the number of customers who had registered with them. Retailers and administrators were warned that these retail permits in no way guaranteed the retailer the supplies needed. Because of the complexity of this, it was decided at a relatively early stage that this aspect of the rationing scheme would best be handled at a local level with local authorities taking the strain.

The division of administrative labour was of prime concern to the sub-committee appointed to plan a rationing system. As was common with food planning, the experiences of the First World War became a template for any future conflict and the initial planning foresaw the need for a central office at the Ministry of Food (MoF), divisional offices (for England, Scotland, Wales and Ireland) below this level, and finally, for an estimated 1,900 local offices. Food committees were to be established within each local authority and the burden of managing the rationing scheme would largely fall upon them. The local offices would not only be expected to administer the scheme but would also be expected to ensure compliance, solve problems (whether of compliance or supply to retailers) and deal with price variations.at a local level.

Sir William Beveridge was the chair of the Sub-Committee on Rationing which proposed the above scheme, but it is clear that he recognised further problems which were beyond the remit of his committee and his report on the potential rationing scheme included a particularly perceptive addendum. In this he outlined four elements which he believed had to be taken into consideration:

1. A Food Controller must be appointed with full powers on the very day that war was declared.
2. A feeding policy for maintaining an adequate supply of food for the entire country had to be thought through in advance of war.
3. A control plan had to be put in place which would enable the government to regulate prices and distribution of essential food stocks as well as administering supply.
4. A plan must be put in place for providing food in the result of aerial attacks.

Beveridge also highlighted the need for secure storage of nutritional food stocks and for the necessity of a network which would allow the stocks to be moved to where they were most required. He also added a list of items which he believed might need to be rationed. Once again, he fell back on the experience of the previous war but was again proven to be correct in his judgements as his extensive list omitted only two items which were later rationed (tea and cooking oil).

It was increasingly clear that the war was going to have a massive impact on agriculture and on the eating and consumption habits of the British people. Greater mechanisation would be needed if farming was to become more efficient, methods of farming would also have to adapt with less livestock farming and greater arable farming. Farmers would also be affected by the price controls which were to be introduced (though in many cases this would actually result in farmers gaining better prices for their produce amidst a guaranteed market). Controls would grow ever greater and more restrictive as the war went on.

Consumers would be affected by the rationing which was to be introduced and refined as the war went on (and for a number of years afterwards). Responsible housekeepers would have to become accustomed to a number of new regimes: queuing; registering with suppliers; carefully shepherding coupons; and with using ever more innovative cooking and preparation methods to both feed their families and preserve what foods were available for as long as possible.

Despite most farming communities attempting to maintain some attempt at normality and routine, the approach to war and the early months of the conflict brought noticeable changes in the routine of rural life. In 1930–31 there had been some 1,353,000 people employed in agriculture in Britain (only two other groups outweighed it – with 2,323,000 employees in commercial occupations in 1930–31, while mining employed some 1,988,000 people), but there had been a drift away from rural areas. This was partly reversed as some young men sought out work on farms in an effort to avoid anticipated conscription. Despite this, there was still an almost immediate shortage of agricultural labour. By the spring of 1940 some 30,000 young men employed in agriculture had joined the forces; almost half were already members of the Territorials and left immediately they were mobilised and others were either called up as reservists or volunteered in order to take part in what they saw as a more exciting profession. Poor pay and conditions also contributed to this exodus as a further 20,000 left the rural areas to seek better paid work elsewhere. During the period of the Phoney War, an agricultural worker earned just £1 17s 10d per week while a man could become an unskilled labourer at one of the many camps and factories which were being built in rural areas and earn double this amount. This caused a rift in parliament as Bevin refused to do anything to stop the drift away from agriculture until the Agricultural Wages Board agreed to bring in a minimum weekly pay rate of £2 8s for agricultural workers. Left with little choice the government agreed to this and in 1941 agricultural work came under the auspices of the Essential Work Order.

Agriculture and the fishing industry had to adapt to shortages of manpower, which meant not only a growing dependence upon mechanisation but also upon the use of alternative sources of labour such as the Women's Land Army (WLA) and by using PoWs (largely Italian) as farm labourers.

Chapter 1

Organised Commercial Agriculture

The Ministry of Agriculture and Fisheries

The most critical bodies governing this area were the Ministry of Agriculture (MoAg) and the Ministry of Food (MoF) (see later). As soon as war was declared, the MoAg shifted its seventeen London-based divisions to their planned wartime duties. Amongst these divisions were those which were devoted to animal feed, tractors and farm implements, with another for fertilisers and feeds. Key to the oversight of wartime agriculture were the War Agricultural Executive Committees (War Ags) which numbered more than a hundred and were organised on a county by county basis and were directly responsible to the Minister of Agriculture. Each War Ag consisted of eight to twelve unpaid volunteers (usually made up of local landowners or farmers) who were assisted by a full-time paid staff of advisers, consisting largely of technical advisers, university professors and land agents. The War Ags divided each county into a number of districts; each had their own boards with each having sub-committees dedicated to various tasks such as animal feed, cultivation, drainage or labour, and so on.

When the war began, there were some 12 million acres of arable land in Britain compared with more than 17 million acres of grassland. The MoAg was keenly aware that for Britain to produce enough food to keep its population going in the event of war, and the likelihood of submarine warfare affecting supply routes across the Atlantic, it would be necessary to massively increase the amount of arable land to produce wheat and potatoes, along with other less valuable crops.

Under the auspices of the MoAG a plethora of new committees and sub-committees came into existence in the event of war. The somewhat complex system of ministries, committees, and sub-committees which sought to govern the growing, harvesting, pricing and distribution of food in wartime Britain was typically British; it was rather cumbersome, but it worked. The planning for agriculture, for example, was already well advanced before the beginning of the war and it became one of the few British success stories of the early months of the war.

Challenges

The effort to feed the nation during wartime would be a huge challenge and although planning had been relatively thorough and well considered, the success of the farming industry in providing enough food and fodder would require farmers to accept the changes and challenges alongside careful management while the challenge of ensuring good supplies and fair shares for all would fall largely upon the MoF.

Farmers were quickly made aware that they were on the front lines of the war. A new raft of ARP measures alongside the introduction of War Ags led to anxiety for many farmers. In particular, there were fears that the War Ags eroded long-held freedoms but the government was also keen to maintain morale amongst the rural population. The Minister of Agriculture, Reginald Dorman-Smith, MP, gave a broadcast on the BBC as early as 4 September 1939 which was almost solely aimed at farmers and farm labourers. In the broadcast he stated that the main aim for farmers was to increase production of essential foodstuffs and that for this to happen the ploughing up of 10 per cent of arable or idle land would be absolutely vital. Initially this land was to be seeded with wheat or potatoes with the possibility of crops of 'oats, barley, beans, peas, rye, or maize'.[1] Dorman-Smith also urged labourers to stay on the land as their efforts were vital to the war effort. In order to appease farmers and labourers the minister said that he would ensure that, as farmers were incurring greater costs, it was only fair that they would also realise decent profits. He added that this would also apply to the farm labourers and, indeed, wages did increase in the first months of the war.

The Ploughing-up Campaign

Although Britain had been the first country to become industrialised it still maintained a large agricultural sector. In 1935, for example, the country produced 1,743,000 tons of wheat, 732,000 tons of barley, and 1,819,000 tons of oats. These figures were dwarfed by the production of 3,765,000 tons of potatoes and a massive 3,346,000 tons of sugar beet.

The ploughing-up campaign, introduced at the start of the war, encouraged and rewarded farmers for ploughing up land and turning it to arable production. Initially, however, it actually resulted in a decline in the amount of wheat produced in 1940 (1,628,000 tons, a fall of 115,000 tons) and in sugar beet (3,120,000 tons, a fall of 226,000 tons), although there were very substantial increases in other produce. Barley production increased to 1,089,000 tons (an increase of 357,000 tons), oats to 2,514,000 tons (an increase of 695,000 tons), and the production of potatoes increased to 5,375,000 tons (a massive increase of 1,610,000 tons). By the end of the war, production showed marked increases. Wheat production stood at 2,174,000 tons, barley at 2,096,000 tons, oats at 2,862,000 tons, sugar beet at 3,783,000 tons and potato production had boomed to 8,702,000 tons (an increase of 4,937,000 tons over the 1935 figure).

All across Britain, farmers were putting meadows and pastures to the plough under the instruction of the MoAg and it was said that every farmer was obsessed to one extent or another with ploughing, preparing to plough or pleading to avoid ploughing up treasured pasture. For the farmers of Britain there was no such thing as the

Phoney War; for them the war began immediately and led to massive changes in their working routines.

Early wartime harvests were excellent due to the fact that much of the newly used arable land, ploughed up due to and repurposed due to government encouragement, had had time to store up great fertility during its barren period. Across Britain, many wartime harvests, boosted by this fertility and the greater acreage of arable land in use, dragged on until almost Christmas. Science could accomplish many things for Britain's farmers but it could not alter the seasons upon which British farming was so dependent. The harvesting of arable crops was hindered by lack of labour, by the frequently awful wartime winters and by wartime events which sometimes saw fields ravaged by bombs or incendiaries. By the later war years, the increased levels of fertility in newly ploughed ground had largely been worn out and new methods were being encouraged by both the MoAg and the local county War Ags. Ley farming, although used widely in Scotland, was to prove a controversial matter despite the proven scientific evidence that it was a useful method of restoring fertility to tired and worn-out soil.

It was not only the supply of food for humans that was of concern at this early stage of the war. Fodder supplies for livestock also had to be maintained and as early as the summer of 1940 the government warned that farmers would be expected to undertake far greater work in the production of arable produce. This warning came out as many farmers were involved in harvesting hay for winter feed. This already involved extra work for some enterprising farmers as many parks and gardens had also been turned over to the production of grass for hay and this too required harvesting. Plymouth had opened its Central Park in 1928 and its large, open, meadows were turned over to production with large amounts of hay being harvested in the summer of 1940.

Livestock farmers had their own problems. Livestock producers had been dependent upon the mass importation of feed with nearly 9 million tons being shipped to Britain every year. The ploughing-up campaign inevitably saw a reduction in livestock on farms with the slaughtering of huge numbers of pigs and poultry (which gave little back to the land from their rearing) during the summer and autumn of 1940. The U-Boat campaigns in the Atlantic and on the East Coast saw a massive reduction in the importation of feed, culminating in just 1,300,000 tons coming in during 1943/44. Some livestock farmers felt somewhat hard done by in the wake of the ploughing-up campaign but the MoAg did its best to defend them against criticism (largely from the MoF) although it was forced to concede that in terms of production per acre livestock farming was inevitably less efficient. In 1942, the MoAg was forced to point out to livestock farmers that not only did arable farming feed many more people per acre but that an acre of wheat grown in Britain saved as much shipping space as 7 acres of grassland.

The campaign continued throughout the war and by 1944 there were 14,500,000 acres under arable crop production in Britain. This represented an increase of almost 6 million acres and came despite the loss of the 800,000 acres commandeered for the building of airfields, camps and factories.

Across Britain, golf courses, bowling greens, school playing fields and public and private parks fell victim to the plough. In south-west England, flower growers turned their land over to potatoes, carrots and wheat. The King's Great Park in Windsor was not immune and became the largest wheat field in Britain. Remarkably unpromising land was also put into production. In Galloway, grassland was ploughed up despite the granite outcrops which were an almost ever-present hazard. The Sussex Downs were put into arable production for the first time in over a thousand years. Drainage of marshlands in Cumberland, Cheshire and of forests in Wiltshire allowed even more land to be utilised for farming. In East Anglia, thousands of acres of fenland were also drained – revealing buried forests which required clearing by the Royal Engineers – and turned into farmland. In the mountains and hills of Wales, bracken and thorns were cleared to make way for the plough. Montgomeryshire managed, through this clearance, to produce enough potatoes to feed the entire city of Manchester. This incredible success would not have been possible without the absolute dedication of the MoAg which handed out large and generous grants to clear land to make way for crops.

The ploughing-up campaign was not without its problems. It skewed British farming towards arable production in a way which had never before been attempted. Later in the war, for example, the government's demand for a much greater production of potatoes resulted in a massive change to farming practice. In the sixth year of the war, the acreage of land producing potatoes had more than doubled, while that producing wheat had increased by 66 per cent. The ploughing-up campaign was one of the home front's great success stories and by 1944 the ratio of arable to grassland had been almost completely reversed. Surveys in this year showed that there were 18 million acres of arable land under the plough and grassland had fallen to just 11 million acres.

New Regulations

One of the more contentious issues dealt with by the MoAg and the MoF was the control of prices of certain commodities. The government became the sole purchaser of wheat, livestock and milk and guaranteed the farming community that it would pay specific prices, equal to those at the outbreak of the war.

Farmers rallied to the cause, many being encouraged to get behind the ploughing-up campaign with the offer of £2 for every acre of grassland that they put to the plough. Despite the grumbling and, in some cases, anger, the initial target was hit by April 1940; this despite the severe weather of winter and a cold spring. Farmers worked seven days a week to hit their targets and some even ploughed at night having obtained special permission to use lamps to aid them. In 1940–1, efforts intensified with almost 2 million acres being ploughed. A further half a million followed in the following year. In the crisis year of 1942, with heavy losses in the Atlantic, farmers were ominously told that they had to redouble their efforts and ignore the possible consequences on production in 1944 or subsequent years that this might involve. By now, however, there was less grassland eligible for the plough along with shortages of labour and the government asked that only 960,000 acres be ploughed. In the event, the farmers responded magnificently and over-achieved, putting 1,376,000 acres to the plough. This effort was enhanced by a long and hot summer in 1943 which brought a record harvest.

The government's urging was a distinctly mixed blessing. Distrust amongst farmers ran rampant. Many had keen memories of the repeal of the Agriculture Act in 1921, despite government promises to guarantee prices of oats and wheat. The result of this had been a catastrophic collapse in prices, with wheat being particularly badly hit. From a 1920 high of 80s 10d per quarter, prices immediately fell to 44s 2d just two years later. Prices of wheat failed to recover and a new low was reached in 1934 when it stood at just 27s 9d. This was the lowest figure since records had been kept in 1646.

The ploughing-up campaign continued throughout the war and by 1944 there was 14,500,000 acres of arable crop production in Britain. This represented an increase of almost 6 million acres and came despite the loss of 800,000 acres which were commandeered for the building of airfields, camps and factories.

Unsurprisingly, the farmers were very wary of government intervention or promises of fixed pricing. Partly as a result of this distrust, mixed with the poor prices and a lack of entrepreneurship and initiative within the farming industry, most British farms had remained outdated. Lack of capital and credit had hindered investment while the inbred conservatism of the majority of farmers resisted many technological and scientific advances. Even in 1943 it was discovered that fewer than half of the farms in England and Wales possessed a running, piped water supply, while only 25 per cent had an electricity supply. The best conditions tended to be found in the

Home Counties while those in Wales, the south-west and other more distant locales were described as primitive.

One result of the collapse in grain prices was that farmers had turned away from arable production and increasingly devoted their efforts to dairy farming. In order to save money, many had instituted a ranch system which led to large areas of former arable land going to waste. On many farms, drainage systems, fencing and hedging had been left go to rack and ruin and large tracts of land had not been limed for many years. Neglect had also spread to roads and housing and many farmers were living in conditions little better than their labourers. Across the whole of Britain there were large expanses of land which had been neglected and allowed to become overgrown.

Aware of the growing crisis, the governments of the 1930s had attempted to alleviate the conditions through a variety of measures including the subsidisation of prices for a number of crops and produce, including cereals, sugar beet, bacon, milk, cheese, sheep and fat cattle. Perhaps the greatest government intervention had been the introduction of various marketing boards which were elected by farmers and which helped control the selling of a number of products such as milk, bacon, potatoes and hops. The most successful of these was probably the Milk Marketing Board and dairy farmers had, by and large, done quite reasonably in the immediate pre-war years. Despite this, the recovery was extremely uneven, and varied from area to area.

The raft of new regulations introduced by the government in the first months of the war impacted on every aspect of the farming and food industries. Regulations covered everything from the rearing of stock, obtaining feed, to the butchery trade. These changes impacted in many large and small ways. In Northumberland, for example, Alnwick's economy was still largely dominated by rural and agricultural affairs, with the cattle market being of great importance to the town. In January 1940, the government notified the council that it would be taking over the running of the slaughterhouse with the MoF paying a specified fee per head of cattle passing through;

in addition to this, the MoF also planned to buy up all fat stock at Alnwick Cattle Mart.

The coming of the new regulations and laws inevitably led to some tensions. In Wales, many farmers had grown increasingly disgruntled with the actions of the London-based National Farmers' Union (NFU). In January 1940, the annual meeting of the Cardiganshire branch grew heated with the members being quite caustic about the growing disjoint with the national committee. Amongst the grievances which were aired at the meeting was the calling up of men under 21, which had deprived many small forms of a crucial supply of labour – but the central complaint was the perception of unfairness in the ploughing-up campaign. The farmers alleged that the ploughing up quota which had been placed upon Cardiganshire was a very heavy one, and that the call-up of men under 21 would result in many farmers being unable to reach their quota. Mr D.J. Davies said that the county had been unfairly treated, it had already ploughed up more land in proportion to its size than any other county and that its reward for this was to be given a quota of 33½ per cent compared to other counties which had been given only 20-25 per cent. Mr Davies claimed that the government had seemed to forget that Cardiganshire had thrown its weight behind the effort to increase milk production and the branch decided that it would protest the ploughing up quota. The anticipated loss of sources of farm labour due to young men joining the forces would, argued the farmers, mean that they would struggle to be as efficient as they already were and that this lack of manpower would in all likelihood see them unable to fulfil their ploughing up quotas.

Another cause of bitter complaint was the government-fixed wool prices. Many farmers in north Cardiganshire depended on the wool price for much of their livelihood and the recent low prices were affecting them badly. One such farmer, Mr Lodwick Evans claimed that the price of wool had stood at 1s 5d per lb in 1938 before falling to 9d in 1939 but that the government was now offering between 8¾d to 11½d at the beginning of 1940. Mr Evans then went on to explain how he had recently purchased a woollen garment for 2s 6d which before the war would only have cost him 1s 11d. When he queried this price he was told it was because of an increase in the price of wool.

A rebuff came from no less than the MP for Cardiganshire, Mr D.O. Evans. Mr Evans claimed that it was essential that the farmers of Britain produce as much food as possible and bluntly told them that regardless of their feelings on such matters, farmers in Cardiganshire, as elsewhere, would have to change their peacetime policies and practices for the national good. He also told them that they should remember that there were severe restrictions on shipping as a result of the war and that the greatest armament of war was adequate food production.

Despite the concerns of the members of the Cardiganshire branch, the vote on forming a separate Welsh NFU was heavily defeated. They may have been disgruntled at the perceived lack of understanding being shown by both the government and by the national committee of the NFU in London but they were equally aware that farmers now found themselves in the front line of the war effort and that to be seen as moaning could result in a perception of a lack of loyalty.

Elsewhere in Wales, the New Year brought other concerns to farmers in the Llanrwst area of Conwy. Here, farmers decided to petition the government to recognise the difference between farmhouse butter and other forms of butter and to raise the price of farmhouse butter to 2s per lb. Local farmers were also greatly concerned that the current butter ration of ¼lb per person per week was insufficient for farm workers who depended upon bread and butter for a large proportion of their diet and who were undertaking vital and heavy manual labour. The farmers asked the government to consider raising the butter ration for all persons involved in heavy industrial work of any nature.

In this they were aided by a benevolent regime at the MoAg. When war broke out the head of the MoAg was Sir Reginald

Dorman-Smith. Dorman-Smith had previously been highly placed in the NFU and so was extremely sympathetic to the farmers. When Churchill replaced Chamberlain as prime minister he appointed Robert Hudson as Minister of Agriculture. Hudson was also sympathetic to the case of the farmers and, in this attitude, he was joined by his two juniors, the Duke of Norfolk and the Labour MP, Tom Williams. The last named was particularly enamoured of the farmers. A former miner, he found common sympathies with the farmers' sense of persecution and went out of his way to retain his popularity with them. Thus, the farmers saw massive financial support throughout the war.

In many ways the war proved to be good for farmers' profits with price controls on many goods ensuring that they received more for their produce than had been the experience of most during the doldrums of the 1930s. In 1938, for example, the average prices per cwt of wheat was 6s 9d, barley at 10s 2d, and oats at 7s 7d. At the height of the war in 1943 the comparable prices were 16s 3d for wheat, 31s 5d for barley and 15s 8d for oats.

This brought some criticism from other industries which believed they were not being treated as leniently or favourably as agriculture was. The simple fact was that the production of food was of such vital importance that Churchill and the government would have gone to almost any lengths to aid farmers and to keep them on side.

Indeed, it can be said that the war was a watershed moment in British farming in that it introduced practices which proved to be of great benefit to the sector in the post-war years. One of the greatest improvements was in the increasing willingness of many, but by no means all, farmers to embrace change – specifically new technologies and science. This change in mentality was aided by the way in which the government went about converting the farmer. There would doubtless have been far greater resistance if the main instrument of instruction had been through the centralised government civil servants of the MoAg but it was instead largely undertaken through the county War Ags. This was far more acceptable as the people who served on the committees tended to be fellow farmers and agriculturalists who, in many cases, were personally known to local farmers.

*****

Feeding Livestock

With the increasingly grim toll taken in the Battle of the Atlantic, there was an ever-greater demand for conservation of livestock feed; the MoAg launched a sustained campaign to remind farmers of this. For Orkney farmers, October 1943 brought a stern reminder not to waste precious stores of winter livestock feed. Although supplies had been maintained, the restrictions on imports and the effects of losses continuing to be suffered in the Battle of the Atlantic meant that such supplies as were available were not to be used for purposes which would have been perfectly normal during pre-war days but were now considered to be squandered resources. For the coming winter, farmers were informed, protein would be in short supply but this would be somewhat balanced by the greater availability of cereals. As with most aspects of wartime Britain the supply of such materials was strongly enforced, and the government issued guidelines for farmers. For dairy cows, for example, 4 units (1 protein and 3 cereal) were to be allotted for every 100 gallons of milk sold in excess of 15 gallons per cow per month. There was, however, a cereal deduction of 48lbs per cow per month, calculated on milk sales from two months previously. This deduction could be waived if 3cwt of oats or dredge corn per cow had been sold. There were a number of adjustments which could be made to these figures for winter milk producers who had a high proportion of autumn and early winter calvers in their herds. For those who kept no more than two cows for producing milk for the household and where no rations were issued per milk sales a monthly allowance of ¼ unit of protein could be applied for.

Those farmers who relied on horsepower for their work were reminded that growing winter feed for these horses was to be a priority but for those farmers who could not produce enough winter feed, rations would be allowed, depending on proof being confirmed, at a maximum of 4 units per horse involved in heavy and continuous work. In addition, a half unit of bran could be secured by the sale of a similar quantity of oats.

For poultry keepers, 1 unit was issued for every 160 birds, while pig keepers (and there were many who became wartime pig keepers) received 1 unit for every 8 pigs. Once again there were deductions. For pigs this deduction was at the rate of 1 unit for every 8 acres while for poultry keepers it was set at 3 units for every 40 acres. Where both pigs and poultry were kept on the same farm the rate was set at 1 unit for every 10 acres. A further ration of 3 units was allowed for each breeding sow or gilt which was about to farrow.

For those growing oats, beans and peas (Orkney farmers, like many others had been encouraged to bring otherwise unproductive land into arable and vegetable production) and who sold such large quantities for seed that they were left with insufficient supplies to feed their own livestock, additional coupons could be applied for in order to enable them to meet the needs of their stock.

The local War Agricultural Committees had previously had quantities of feed placed under their charge for issuance at their own discretion but farmers were informed that in 1943 this quantity would be substantially reduced and that protein, in particular, would be in very short supply. Farmers were warned that, although the War Ags would make every attempt to satisfy demand it might not be possible and that, in some situations, applications which were worthy might even have to be turned down due to lack of supplies.

By 1943/44 there was a shift detectable in government policy. Ploughing-up had been a massive success and a further 600,000 acres were ploughed up during this year but there was a shift back towards the necessity of expanding livestock production once more. This resulted in a return to pasture for some recently ploughed land but livestock farmers had become much more efficient as a result of the first years of the war and it was now possible for them to rear larger numbers of cattle on less land than had previously been the case.

The Ministry of Food

One of the measures to manage the nation's food supplies during war, which had been put in place well in advance of the war, was the establishment of a department specifically dedicated to the matter. The Food (Defence Plans) Department was formed in May 1936 as part of the Board of Trade but there were some cautious plans to expand the department into a ministry in the event of a prolonged war. Typically, the government entered into the project in a half-hearted manner and it did not even announce the creation of the new department until seven months after it had been formed.

The director of the new department was the second secretary in the MoAg, Henry French (to become Sir Henry in 1938). French was far from the typical faceless civil servant as he was unafraid to make public pronouncements or speaking to the press and he went on to become, as the wartime private secretary of the MoF, one of the most important people in the matter of food supply in wartime Britain.

The new department faced constant criticism and scepticism in the years from its founding to the beginning of the war (and beyond) with the traditional agricultural lobby groups being suspicious of the department and its impact as they feared a loss of their own influence over the MoAg. French was a skilled diplomat but even he could achieve only so much, and the suspicions remained. Much of the parliamentary displeasure resulted from circumstances which were beyond the control of Sir Henry or his department and were in fact symptoms of the Chamberlain government's inertia, vacillation and unwillingness to spend money. One of the most serious of these issues was the lack of storage facilities which had been made available for the storage of vital supplies during the war. The necessity had been highlighted on multiple occasions, beginning with Beveridge, but the government had refused to countenance the increase in spending on numerous occasions.

The government, easily criticised for many of its failures to prepare for war, actually did fairly well in responding to Beveridge's concerns. The issue of food control was taken over by the Ministry of Food (MoF) and its minister, William Morrison. It rapidly adjusted to wartime conditions, its divisions benefiting from the advice of some of the leading businessmen in Britain at the time. For example, Sir Francis Boys, the vice-chair of the Livestock Commission, was made the trade representative for meat and livestock, while an unnamed director of Lever Brothers undertook a similar project with regard to oils and fats. Morrison was also aided by economics, statistics, and intelligence divisions. The two ministries worked hand-in-glove with one another but while the far-longer established MoAg had some 3,500 staff, the newcomer MoF had only 375. One of the first tasks of the MoF, therefore, was to undertake a massive recruitment drive to bolster its numbers and by March 1940 the number of staff had risen to 3,500.

In a similar manner to the MoAg, the MoF also had a large local organisation with nineteen divisional officers around the whole of Britain. These officers were responsible for the activities of the 1,400 or so local food control committees which were organised broadly along council lines. Each committee had fifteen members and it was firmly stipulated that at least one-third of these members should be made up of local tradespeople, with the remaining ten members representing local consumer interests in various ways. Normally each had a trade unionist and a representative from the Women's Institute (WI). These food committees were largely tasked with ensuring that sufficient supplies of food reached local shops, and with the preparations for and the control of rationing when it was implemented in January 1940.

Once again, the pre-war preparations served the government well and the two most important Departments were closely linked.

The Dangers of Being Bombed

Many of the cities of Britain were, by necessity, surrounded by a wide rural hinterland which supplied them with food. This and the shortcomings of navigation in the Luftwaffe exposed those in these rural areas to danger from enemy bombing. Admittedly it was not as great a danger as that faced by those living in urban areas but enemy bombing could still inflict casualties and often destroyed precious crops. There were many incidents where bombs destroyed valuable crops, killed livestock, destroyed farm buildings and equipment and in some cases killed people.

One of the earliest examples of this occurred in March 1940. A raid over Orkney captured the attention of the nation and demonstrated clearly how rural communities were also exposed to the dangers of aerial warfare. Two farms at Stenness also received damage, largely through incendiary bombs. At one of these farms the farmer, Mr James Donaldson, and his family successfully fought a fire which had been started by an incendiary bomb falling on a shed. Showing great courage and fortitude the Donaldson family fought the fire while the raid continued around them.

For the stunned residents of Stenness there was little to be excited about. Mr John Isbister, a blacksmith and son of a farmer and the brother-in-law of a man who was killed, described the night's events to the *Orkney Herald*. Describing it as an evening which he would never forget, he told the reporter that 'it is difficult for us to realise that such terrible things have been happening in Stenness'. Mr Isbister described how his first intimation of the raid came at around 8 p.m. when he heard the unmistakable sound of German aircraft. Stepping out of his home he immediately saw a German bomber pass low overhead and saw and heard anti-aircraft fire from the direction of Scapa. After a time, the firing slackened off somewhat and Mr Isbister, believing the raid was passing, went down to check on his workshop at Bridge of Waithe. As he passed the cottages he noticed that some of the residents had come out to watch the raid and they exchanged remarks 'about it being an exciting night'. Suddenly the firing grew more intensive and Mr Isbiston went back to his farm at Upper Onston, a few hundred yards from Bridge of Waithe. He had only just made it back under cover when he heard aircraft once more. Shortly afterwards there was a series of loud explosions quite close by and he observed flashes of fire through the windows. At the neighbouring farm of Queena several haystacks caught fire after being hit by incendiary bombs. Seconds later there was a series of explosions which sounded as if they were just outside and which 'shook the house to its foundations' and caused the children to scream.

In another early incident, shortly after 11 p.m. on 26 June 1940, the people of County Durham and Sunderland were awoken by the wail of the air raid sirens as approximately 100 enemy aircraft were detected crossing the Scottish and north-east coast. Shortly after midnight a high explosive bomb exploded at Witherwack Farm, Southwick, but this resulted in no casualties or significant damage. Meanwhile, fifty incendiary bombs fell on the village green at Whitburn. Others fell onto a haystack and a house but no damage was done.

Farmers received advice from a great many sources during the war. Some of this advice came from the authorities in control of ARP. Although admitting that farms were usually amongst the safest places to be during bombing, the authorities did give Northumberland farmers some initial advice on actions to be taken in the event of bombs being dropped on their land. In the event of gas attack, farmers were advised that byres and other buildings used to house livestock could be rendered reasonably gas-proof by shutting all doors and windows, closing ventilators and by hanging damp sacking over them. To prevent damage from blast bombs, farmers were advised to sandbag their buildings to a height of approximately 6 feet. Few did. Acknowledging that enemy bombers could jettison bombs over farmland, and with the fear of chemical attack to the fore, farmers were advised that any gas bombs dropped should be reported immediately and that animals should be kept away from the area. Furthermore, animals which had been splashed by mustard gas or lewisite should be wiped clean with a rag soaked in paraffin or petrol and bleach applied for five minutes followed by a paste of bleaching powder and water. If the eyes were affected they were to be washed with a bicarbonate of soda solution. All animal feeds which were in the open as well as any open-roofed buildings should be covered by tarpaulins while stores of grain should be covered with a material which was not easily ignitable. Farmers were also given the advice which applied to other households: to cover windows with strips of cellulose in order to prevent them shattering.

British farming, however, was by its nature mixed and the demand for more arable production caused an imbalance in many areas. The need to retain mixed farming also had practical reasons. The government demanded that milk production be maintained and thus the traditional mixed farm continued to rear cattle. Indeed, the number of cattle in Britain actually increased during the war. Milk production, however, fell slightly. In the middle of the war it was some 4 per cent below pre-war totals. Investigations showed that there had been a steep decline in yield per beast but this fall was in large part due to the shortage of concentrated feed.

The concentration on arable production resulted in a sharp decline in other forms of produce. In 1943/44, beef and veal output fell by a sixth, mutton and lamb by a fifth, eggs by 50 per cent and pork products by 66 per cent.

Mixed and livestock farmers with remaining pasture were encouraged to experiment with ley farming. This involved the sowing of arable land with temporary grasses and was a method which had found favour with agricultural scientists and had been extensively used in Scotland before the war. Ley farming, farmers were repeatedly told, restored tired soil while the fertility of former grassland allowed bumper arable crops to be grown. Ley farming, however, was a controversial method and the arguments over it continued throughout the war. Many more conservative farmers looked on it askance and extolled the virtues of retaining old pasturelands.

More open-minded farmers began experimenting with alternative feeding methods. Greater use of silage was another method which generated extensive debate amongst farmers. Some farmers who extolled the method even began experimenting with their own mixtures and some improvised their own silos using whatever was at hand or obtainable. Silos made from old iron tanks, wire and cardboard and even railway sleepers lined with newspaper were all tried across the country.

With the growing importance of securing the national food supply in the face of ongoing submarine and anti-shipping warfare in the Atlantic and on the East Coast, the government and local authorities were keen to make sure that the agricultural sector increased its productivity and maintained the morale of its workforce. In early June, agricultural labourers received the welcome news that their wages were to be increased to a minimum of 48s per week. The move was enthusiastically backed by branches of the NFU across the country and the union leaders stated that they were determined to make the policy a success by increasing production for the national effort.

As 1940 continued, the business of auction marts around the county continued. In mid-September the well-known Rothbury based firm of Robert Donkin Ltd holding a cash sale of 7,500 lambs. These lamb sales were of huge importance for the hill farmers of many areas of upland Britain, including large parts of Northumberland, Cumberland, Yorkshire and Scotland. These hill farmers faced distinct challenges which varied from those of their colleagues who farmed in more hospitable areas of the country.

For farmers in many parts of upland Britain, the ploughing-up campaign took second place due to the unsuitability of the ground. Some farmers protested against being ordered to plough up ground which they believed was unsuitable for arable production. In North Northumberland, for example, much of the terrain was unsuitable and the breeding and rearing of livestock, particularly sheep and cattle, continued to be very extensive. In October 1942, the Livestock Auction Mart Company in Wooler held its annual sale of cross-Angus and shorthorn suckled calves. The sale attracted a catalogue of 650 head with the show said to be of a high standard – many cattle being of exceptional breeding and condition. As a result of this, business was very brisk and the sellers were well pleased with the prices. The highest price received for cross-Angus suckled calves was £20 which was paid to three separate farms (Wrangham, Ingram and Low Hedgeley).

In the same month as the above sale the annual sale of young bulls, milk cows, heifers and suckled cows was held at Rothbury in Northumberland by the firm of Messrs Robert Donkin Ltd. Once again business was very good but there were few suckled calves offered for sale (perhaps as a result of the earlier sale at Wooler). A young bull from Fairley fetched a price of £30 while others fetched £28 (Carterside) and £24 (Tosson Tower). The prices paid for milk cows were also buoyant with one in-calf cow from the nearby farm of Hepple Whitefield fetching the sum of £68 while a calved milk cow from Lorbottle Steads sold at £59. Prices for calved and in-calf heifers were also well received and fluctuated between £29 and £45 10s. Demonstrating the fact that many amateurs were now also dabbling in the rearing of livestock, the Coquetdale Calf Club sold five dairy heifers for prices between £10 and £21.

These successful markets, however, were not the usual. By the summer of 1943, these same markets were reporting that their profits were being stifled by the government's controlled prices. At the start of August, Berwick's cattle market had 118 cattle available for sale but there was only a fair demand with the highest price being £36 for a polled bullock. Despite the concerns of farmers and market officials, many of the fluctuations appear to have been largely seasonal. Just one month after the sale at Berwick came a highly successful lamb sale at Wooler Mart when over 2,700 head were sold. Other parts of the country were reporting lower sales than normal but at this sale there was a sustained demand and prices were higher than the previous year; possibly helped by the high quality of the stock.

At the same time, Berwick Corn Market was reporting that it had very low supplies with commensurately low attendance. Indeed, there were only three suppliers in attendance and all the sales were at prices controlled by the government. Barley sold from 26s 3d to 27s 6d oats for 14s to 14s 9d and wheat for 14s 6d.

With controlled prices and high demand, the many farmers who considered the future realised that this phenomenon was one which could be exploited.

The use of fertilisers saw a significant increase during the war. Many farmers had, of course, already been convinced of the benefits of fertilisers but their better income allowed them to buy fertilisers where they had previously been out of their reach. Throughout the conflict, farmers were bombarded with messages extolling the virtues of new fertilisers and scientific techniques. Despite the fact that farming in Britain was still largely a practice informed solely by tradition and advice handed down from father to son, things were changed by the war. Although it was estimated that approximately only 3 per cent of farmers had attended any formal educational course in farming, the wartime campaigns saw many farmers become more open-minded to agricultural science.

Calder gives an example of this by describing the experiences of a land girl in a Cambridgeshire village. One of the local farmers had allowed his cows to be impregnated artificially by the MoAg but, at first, local opinion was firmly against this new science. Many of the older farmers and farmhands saw it as being against nature and preferred the traditional use of the bull. The first artificially inseminated cow, however, gave birth to a healthy and fine heifer and opinion changed overnight as the farmers and agricultural workers saw how the new science could relieve them of the onerous and sometimes dangerous task of putting the cows to the bull.[2]

Many farmers, especially those living in very remote areas, were already faced with severe transport issues; the war exacerbated these. On many of the Scottish Isles, for example, the traditional rural economies faced new and unexpected challenges but residents made their best attempt to cope and to carry on with the lives they knew. On Orkney the rural economy continued throughout the war although the farmers and crofters faced additional difficulties in getting their produce to market on mainland Scotland. Many sent livestock to three Aberdeen firms. Auctioneers Reith & Anderson Ltd held auctions every Friday at Kittybrewster Auction Mart in Aberdeen regularly dealt with Orkney livestock. Another popular mart was the City Auction Mart in Aberdeen where the long-established firm of John Duncan & Son Ltd held sales three times a week. The other Aberdeen firm was that of Alexander Middleton & Son Ltd. This firm held its sales at what it claimed was the oldest established market in the north of Scotland, Belmont Auction Mart. Further south, Thomas Dickson & Sons advertised for hides, sheepskins, wool and tallow and its adverts told Orcadians that special attention and prices applied for Orkney and Shetland hides.

Hill Sheep and Hill Cattle Grazing Scheme

We have already seen that the controlled prices were enabling many lowland farmers to make large profits but for those in upland areas there was growing resentment. Livestock farmers in Northumberland (and especially the upland areas where hill-farming was the usual) complained that making a profit was far more difficult for the hill farmers who had to depend largely upon sheep and was, therefore, considerably affected by the vagaries of the weather (which for the last few years had seen appalling winters). The government responded to these complaints and in 1943 introduced the Hill Sheep and Hill Cattle Grazing Scheme. This scheme had three main aims: to financially help the hill farmers; to preserve the breeding flocks of hill and mountain sheep; and to make greater use of hill land for the national interest. The scheme, however, had been designed largely for farmers in the more mountainous terrain of Scotland and Wales and many Northumberland hill farmers were greatly angered to find themselves excluded from the scheme because their land was not above 800 metres.

Throughout the war, most local and national newspapers ran regular columns on agriculture and horticulture aimed at professional farmers and the enthusiastic amateur. In May 1941, the *Morpeth Herald* ran an article praising the efforts already made by the farming community in restoring great swathes of land to productivity; it claimed that 3,750,000 acres had been ploughed up and that the percentage of productive crop acres had increased from a pre-war 28 per cent to 40 per cent. The article went on, however, to state that some farmers still seemed to be lagging and were not taking the national situation seriously enough. It claimed that the uptake of the ample supplies of nitrogen and sulphate fertilisers made available by the government remained very poor.

Farmers were also encouraged to make use of catch crops instead of allowing their land to lie fallow for long periods between main crops. The article went on to urge farmers to use harvested land for the growing of green fodder crops such as kale, Italian rye grass or green turnips to replace lost grazing land which had been ploughed up.

Despite the clear fact that farmers were making a valuable contribution to the war effort, there was an increasingly commonly held view that farmers had already been coddled by the government and by the various marketing boards and there was considerable resentment towards the farmers from some sections of the public. The belief that farmers were doing extremely well out of the war was to some extent correct. In 1942, it was estimated that farmers' incomes had increased by 207 per cent during the war and agricultural workers' wages by some 61 per cent. This was compared to an increase of 42 per cent for those in manufacturing while general net income had increased by 35 per cent. The undoubted increase in profits for farmers was not even across the board, with dairy farmers, for example, seeing small increases. The main benefactors were the arable farmers, some of whom saw immense profit margins, and the perennially ill-funded hill sheep farmers.

Clearly, the government were aware of the profits being made by farmers and there was increasing concern over the fact that some farmers were clearly becoming used to this government support and were increasingly seeing it as their right. Farmers also benefited from the fact that poor record-keeping often meant the government were unable to claw back some of the money from income tax. The belief that farmers increasingly saw these wartime privileges as rights was reinforced in 1942 when the annual price review failed to take into account an increase in the wages of agricultural workers. In the summer of the following year, workers received another increase and Hudson failed to knuckle under and cover it using the price review. There was immediate anger amongst the farmers and meetings at which angry speeches took place across many areas of the country, attacking Hudson and the government. Hudson failed to quell this discontent and, in fact, made it worse with his lack of tact when dealing with the enraged farmers. Such was the power of the farmers by this stage of the war, however, that the government was forced into making some minor concessions to appease them and agreed to extend the price guarantees and the assured markets to the summer of 1948. This clearly demonstrated not only the power which the farmers had over the government during the war but also the fact that there was a growing sense of entitlement and militancy amongst many British farmers.

Despite this short period of discontent, the war had a remarkable effect on the farming industry which was not solely limited to increased mechanisation but extended to the mental attitude of farmers. Previously, farmers had been considered headstrong, prideful and, in many cases, hidebound to traditions. The war changed this and converted many British farmers to the benefits of state control of the farming industry. The war conditioned farmers to accept being told what to grow, where to grow crops, what to produce, how to go about selling their produce and at what price to sell. The wartime largesse of the government towards farmers came with conditions. One of these was that farmland must now be seen as being not primarily belonging to the farmer but being held in trust for the nation as a whole and that the farm was to be treated as a wartime factory, to be used however the government thought best and, therefore, at the full disposal of the government in terms of how it was utilised. Farmers still complained of the endless form-filling that the war brought but this was more than balanced out by the fact that the war had brought large profits.

While farmers were counting their increased profits their workers also found themselves in a previously unknown position of increased power and influence. The classification of agricultural work as being under the Essential Work Order meant that they had unwarranted power. Traditionally, the workers had been open to victimisation as farmers resentment towards unionisation had kept them in a weak position. The initial shortage of labour, however, meant that the workers could now call some of the shots. One reflection of this was in the fact that membership of the National Union of Agricultural Workers was able to triple its membership between 1938 and 1947. By this last year there were some 163,000 members. Able to bargain a pay rise in the summer of 1940, the workers were then to see further rises in November 1941 (to £3 per week) and June 1943 (to £3 5s) while the rate of pay for overtime was also increased.

Labour

Shortage of labour was also a problem. Although agricultural labourers were reserved at just 21 years of age (and call-up was postponed in any case), the previous decades of low wages and poor, often primitive, living conditions, combined with the greater attractions of higher paid work in the towns and cities, had led to a flight from the country which led to agriculture losing labour at an estimated rate of some 10,000 workers every year between the wars.

In some areas the job market for agricultural labourers was rather itinerant in nature with labourers hiring on to individual farmers for periods of six months or a year. The hiring fairs in which farmers found these workers were commonplace in Northumberland, parts of Scotland and other isolated locations. In Northumberland, they were held in several of the market towns in the county. Many of the farmers preferred men who would also bring along with them women who would serve as extra labour. In exchange for their labour, the workers were paid and also received accommodation and, often, a garden plot and supply of seeds.

Despite the impending war, the annual Morpeth hiring fair for agricultural workers went ahead on 6 March 1939. There was a good attendance and it was reported that a fair amount of business was done but that many of the people who attended had already found work through newspaper advertisements and that many of them, and townspeople, only attended because of the covered fair which took place in the New Market Place.

These hiring fairs were often likened to slave markets but in fact the arrangement suited many agricultural labourers as it meant that their skills were in constant demand and that they could bargain to obtain better pay and working conditions. The system of the hiring fairs, however, was not ideal in wartime as farmers could not always be sure of how much labour they might have available to them.

While 1940 had many reasons for concern among the people of Britain with the Dunkirk Evacuation, the Battle of Britain and the looming possibility of invasion, the government was also concerned that the harvest of 1940 be safely and efficiently brought in so that the nation might be fed.

As the Battle of Britain began to occupy attention and with Britain in a perilous situation it was essential that food supplies be maintained. The harvest saw the drafting in of even larger numbers of volunteers than usual, amongst them many women and children. Local schools in Edinburgh and the surrounding area volunteered to supply labour for the gathering of the harvest and to ensure the supply of food during this time of great crisis. Amongst them were the prestigious Loretto School from Musselburgh with entire classes of boys volunteering their time and sacrificing their afternoon cricket matches and, in some cases, their summer holidays

Once again learning from the previous war, in addition, farmers were informed that some soldiers would be made available for harvest labour. In Northumberland, interested farmers were told that they should apply to the Executive Officer at Bolton Hall. It was also hoped that a number of council employees (mainly road workers) would also come forward to act as harvest labourers and farmers would be advised of this (farmers were also asked to give the names of any such men that they knew to the Executive Officer).

Although more agricultural workers were being recruited by the mid-point of the war, farmers were still complaining of the lack of available labour due to many men now joining the forces. The WLA helped in this respect but there were still shortages in many areas. In the north-east of England, the local papers were filled with advertisements for agricultural workers of all types. The *Newcastle Journal* of 22 January 1943, for example, featured 115 advertisements for agricultural labourers. These varied widely and those in Northumberland included: a byreman (and accompanying woman) to milk a dairy herd at Brandon White House, Powburn; an elderly man or a young lad or woman for general farm work at East Fenton; and a steward, tractor man, two horsemen and a boy and woman to work in the house at Windy Law, Chathill.

Shortages of labour, however, continued to be a problem throughout the war. At the outset there were some 546,000 male workers regularly employed in agriculture along with 55,000 women. These regular workers were joined by some 111,000 casual workers. Recruitment to the forces and other factors quickly denuded the regular workforce and even as late as the summer of 1944, when such work had been classed as 'essential' for some four years) there were just 522,000 men classed as being regularly employed in agriculture, a fall of 24,000 (4 per cent). This was balanced out, however, by the presence of 80,000 members of the WLA and over 90,000 other workers. This meant that although the number of full-time male agricultural workers had declined, the numbers working on the land had increased by 150,000. This would seem to imply that the situation was improving but these extra 150,000 workers were mainly inexperienced and there was therefore a corresponding decline in the overall efficiency of the workforce, albeit this was itself balanced to an extent by greater mechanisation.

Amongst this number by 1943 were some 40,000 Italian PoWs. Part-time help came from a variety of sources including British soldiers and American GIs as well as civilians. Camps for schoolchildren were quickly set up during harvest time and proved popular with many, delighted at the pocket money that could be earned. Other camps were later set up and by 1943 there were 155 adult camps scattered across Britain. Adults could pay a small charge for their accommodation and would know that they were aiding the war effort. This quickly became a popular solution for those seeking some form of vacation and those who went to the camps (and they ranged across all the social spectrum) soon realised that the small fee was quickly recouped by their pay. Alongside these more permanent arrangements were the weekend clubs which cycled out to the countryside and helped work on the farms for the weekend before returning home.

The WLA was not a new idea. The organisation had been created, albeit on a far smaller scale, during the First World War and reformed in 1939 when war appeared increasingly unavoidable. Even so, the initial recruiting campaign was small and unambitious and by the beginning of the war there were just 1,000 members. Although termed an army, the WLA did not have military discipline and all the women were volunteers who could leave if they wished (although they would then usually be eligible to be assigned to other employment on the Essential Work Order or to the auxiliary services such as the WAAF). There was no formal discipline with the only disciplinary procedure being dismissal from the WLA. Land girls were granted a week's leave per year (compared with twenty-eight days in the military) but were given a 'uniform' consisting of brown breeches and slouch hat, khaki overcoat and the ubiquitous green jersey. Given the independent spirit of the members of the WLA, members were not obliged to wear the uniform and many did not or added their own touches to the dowdy clothes.

Organised along local lines, the WLA achieved popularity and influence depending largely upon its local leadership. In

Northumberland at this time of crisis, the WLA quickly achieved popularity and across the area local group leaders were quickly selected: for example, Mrs Weeks of Thirston House was appointed as local recruiting officer for the Felton area and advertised that she was available to give particulars to any interested parties.

Attitudes towards the members of the WLA varied widely. Many farmers were at first suspicious and doubtful over what contribution these, often inexperienced, women could actually make on a farm while some of the countrywomen resented the intrusion of outsiders on their domain. By 1941, however, attitudes were changing and most had come to recognise that the WLA was making a substantial contribution to the nation's agricultural war effort. In April of that year, for example, the *Farmer and Stockbreeder* commented that, despite an initial lack of skill or strength the women made up for this with their zeal and enthusiasm and that the WLA had become 'an indispensable feature of the war effort'. The article went on to admit that not all of the women were suitable for farm work but that the discerning farmer could still find uses for these volunteers in ways which still made a contribution.[3]

Once they had overcome the initial suspicion (and hostility), the WLA quickly found favour and a massive recruitment drive was launched. By the summer of 1941 there were almost 20,000 members and, following this period, women could be directed to serve in the WLA. This conscription, however, was a double-edged sword. Although it brought in more members it also brought in recruits who were far more apathetic in their attitude and dedication towards their duties.

The women of the WLA found themselves used in a wide variety of ways. The catch-all term of horticulture employed many (although they were employed only on the understanding that they were being used in the production of food). One controversial use of a small number of the WLA was in being used to compensate for the shortage in the numbers of gardeners in large private houses and estates. Once again, they were supposed to be employed only in duties which involved food production, but in 1943 the members of the WLA were withdrawn from this role and redeployed into more traditional agriculture. Other duties included rat-catching, at which some of the more enthusiastic members excelled, and in the WLA's own Timber Corps. Those finding themselves in this corps attracted the nickname of lumberjills and faced initial strong doubts over their physical capabilities in the roles. Some 6,000 women eventually served as lumberjills with duties such as tree-felling, operating sawmills, and selecting trees for use as poles. This last role could be an extremely lonely one with a young woman forced to live in rough billets and tramp thousands of miles through rough and lonely country. Other members of the WLA helped in the reclamation of thousands of acres of land from marshes, fens, forests and hillsides.

The vast majority of the WLA, however, were employed on farms. Members of the WLA had to be mobile as they could be shifted from one area to another and had to be prepared to undertake any work they were assigned. Many worked in gangs under the auspices of the county War Ags; by 1943 a third were working in such gangs. Homesickness was a common problem, especially when young women from the north were sent to the Home Counties or vice-versa. WLA gangs were billeted in hostels (either especially built or requisitioned) where they were often closely monitored for any decline in morals. Many of these gangs were employed in threshing work. This was an onerous though essential duty and those thus employed found that the atmosphere was both dirty and noisy and the dust involved ruined the complexion.

The majority of members of the WLA found themselves assigned to work for individual farmers and while this worked in the majority of cases there could be, and were, problems. Accommodation was often cramped and bleak, the hours long, and pay was not linked to the increases in that of agricultural workers. Some farmers, their families and workers were welcoming but others resented the presence of these incomers. Members of the WLA could appeal for higher wages or better conditions, but in a significant number of cases the local representative of the WLA sided with the farmer, whom she often knew personally.

Many farmers initially employed their land girl(s) in milking duties. The job was not a particularly difficult one to learn but boring due to its repetitiveness, and the dirt involved appalled many land girls. Others quickly took to the work and came to enjoy it. The presence of a land girl could also have a destabilising effect on local farmworkers. Language on the farm tended by industrial and many male workers, initially at least, felt somewhat inhibited in the presence of a land girl. Most, however, quickly came to an understanding and many land girls found themselves welcomed, even if sometimes somewhat patronisingly, into the fold.

Some land girls proved themselves to be just as skilled, if not more so, than many of the men whom they were working alongside. In 1941, Miss Betty G.R. Reid, a land girl employed on the Leven, Fife, farm of Mr Arthur Hutchinson, entered the annual ploughing competition of the Scottish National Association of Young Farmers' Clubs. Betty (20) was from the border town of Peebles but was inexperienced in the heavier farm work, although she had attended Edinburgh University to study agriculture. She joined the WLA at the very start of the war and, unsurprisingly, quickly become keenly interested in her work. Betty was in fact one of three members of the WLA to enter the competition and all three had chosen to plough with horses rather than tractors. She later stated that she loved working with horses; other land girls ploughed with the more modern tractors. Miss Reid had at first worked on a dairy farm in Lanarkshire and had gained experience with both horses and stock but ploughing was relatively new to her. The young land girl had not forgotten her ambitions, however, and fully intended to go back to complete her degree once the war was over. Betty Reid went on to defeat many opponents and finished with a hugely creditable overall second place. In the year following her triumph, a short propaganda and recruitment film was made by the WLA which featured the young Scot.

Although the majority of farmers would admit that the women of the WLA proved themselves capable of most tasks it had to be admitted that, while the women could match or even do better than men when undertaking lighter tasks such as caring for poultry or pulling peas, they were less efficient at some tasks such as milking, lifting potatoes and turning hay. It was also admitted that in tasks aided by machinery or by horsepower some women could more than hold their own, as demonstrated by the successes of a number of women in ploughing competitions. By the end of the war farmers agreed that in more labour-intensive tasks three women were worth just two men.

Airfields and Defences

One unfortunate consequence of the war was that a large amount of land was needed for the construction of new airfields. This land was to be found in every part of Britain but the largest proportion were in the eastern counties of Lincolnshire, Yorkshire and East Anglia where the airfields for the growing strength of Bomber Command swallowed huge amounts of farmland. It meant many unfortunate farmers had to give up their precious land. Others lost their land to factories. In the spring of 1940, for example, 100 farmers, smallholders and cottagers on a 2,400-acre estate in North Wales saw their land commandeered for the building of a factory which would employ 10,000 people.

In East Fife, there were plans to build a large naval air station for the use of the Fleet Air Arm and RAF Coastal Command at Balcomie. By the end of July 1939, the proposal had divided opinion in the area. The local MP, Mr J. Henderson Stewart, was a keen supporter but visited the area to assess public opinion. One of the prime movers for the construction of the airfield was a well-known local man named Aird who wrote to the prime minister to advise him that an aerodrome had been placed at Crail during the First World War and that the location was ideal. Some locals believed that the construction might bring economic benefits; others believed that the presence of the airfield would be injurious to the area's tourist trade. For the farmers who were to have their land taken through compulsory purchase there were additional worries. Obviously, the farmers were concerned over the loss of income. One or two pointed out that they had bought the land when prices were at an all-time high and they were concerned as to what compensation would be set at amidst continuing negotiations. Another concern amongst the farmers was that the proposed date for the farmers vacating the land; 1 September 1939 did not allow enough time for the farmers to harvest their current crops and this would cause a further loss of income.

With war declared on 3 September 1939 it took just days for the question of the treatment of farmers to be raised in parliament. On 8 September, the Compensation (Defence) Bill was passed through the house and this prompted several questions from a number of members. The Bill allowed the government to take possession of land and sought to regularise the standard for compensation fees in a fair manner. Lord Apsley, Conservative MP for Bristol Central, intervened to make the point that a case which seemed to highlight inadequacies in this scheme had recently been brought to his attention. One farmer had some 60 acres of his 300-acre farm taken over for the construction of an airfield. The land taken included the two paddocks which were vital for the successful ongoing working of the entire farm and also included the main water supply. The scheme as outlined seemed to be vague when it came to assessing such cases and Lord Apsley asserted that the farmer in question would be forced to leave the farm because it was unworkable. Another case he highlighted involved a farmer whose entire farm was taken over by the Air Ministry. The farmer had been 'turned out lock, stock and barrel, in a great hurry', was homeless, and had not seen a penny in compensation thus far. He had been forced to find alternative accommodation and had used his savings to pay off the interest on loans which he had borrowed from the bank at a rate of 5 per cent. In conclusion, Lord Apsley said that if Sir John Simon (the Chancellor of the Exchequer) went amongst the farmers of the West Country 'he would find quite a lot of bitterness against the Defence Departments concerned relating to the money paid in compensation for farms'.[4]

Following the evacuation of the BEF from Dunkirk, the possibility of invasion loomed large and for many farmers this led to further disruption as a hurried series of defences were erected. The majority of these were in the south-east of England but the defensive lines eventually stretched up the country into northern Scotland. Farmers were forced to give up land so that trenches could be dug, pillboxes constructed and other defences put in place. The vast majority of farmers simply accepted this inconvenience, such was the seriousness of the situation at the time.

As the war went on it became clear that there would be a massive expansion of the RAF and further farmland would need to be requisitioned for the purpose of building new airfields both for the active-duty squadrons and for the training units. While farmers were compensated, the levels of compensation were a constant source of concern for the farming community. Most farmers seem to have been relatively content to (hopefully temporarily) give up their land or at least some of it for the war effort but others were most assuredly not happy. Towards the end of August 1940, the MP for Bedford, Sir Richard Wells, raised the issue in the House. Sir Richard began by informing the Air Minister that he had information that good farming land in his constituency was to be taken for the construction of an airfield and sought assurances that the compulsory purchase of farmland for such construction would take place only after there had been consultation with experts from the MoAg. He was told that arrangements were already in place to see that such consultation did indeed take place.

Many of the farmers who had lost land due to airfield construction sought alternative land to replace that which had been requistitioned. By 1942, many auctioneers and estate agents were taking on farmer clients who were seeking new land. A typical example of this was the advert in the *Rugby Advertiser* of 8 May 1942 in which a farmer who had been dispossessed by airfield construction sought land in the Daventry-Byfield district, through the firm of Holloway, Price & Co.

As the people of Britain became ever more aware of the importance to the war effort of the agricultural community, there was increasing concern over how the farming community was being treated. In October, Lord Woolton addressed 3,000 farmers at Denbigh. Part of his speech was an attempt to allay some of these concerns that were now starting to make headlines in the newspapers.

Shortly after Lord Woolton's speech, the *London Weekly Dispatch* highlighted a case in East Anglia where a site covering hundreds of acres had been taken over by the Air Ministry in 1940. Two years later, the Air Ministry had decided that the land was unsuitable for the proposed construction and the commandeered land was derequisitioned. This had caused some protests from the farmers concerned as workmen had, for two years, been cutting down hedges, clearing ditches and digging drainage for the proposed runways and this meant that the land was being returned to the farmers in far worse condition. The local agricultural community was further angered when the Air Ministry peremptorily announced that it was now considering the requisition of some 400 acres of highly cultivated arable land on the other side of the road. The six farmers whose land would be affected by this new acquisition were understandably angered at imminently being given notice to quit their land. As a result, a special committee meeting was organised at the local branch of the NFU. In covering the story, the press patriotically stated that the needs of the RAF must come first but also questioned the rather off-hand manner in which the farmers were being treated and asked that the Air Ministry explain their actions more clearly.

Fishing

At the start of the war the British fishing fleet had been denuded of vessels and men with many trawlers being commandeered for service as minesweepers or anti-submarine warfare duties and many of the fishermen being members of the Royal Navy Reserve (RNR). Germany had made great play of the fact that with the British commandeering trawlers Britain would be starved of the fish upon which it depended. This proved not to be the case and supplies of fresh fish continued to be landed despite the huge dangers faced by the trawlers which were open to being sunk by mines and which were often attacked by the Luftwaffe.

Where possible the Royal Navy tried to leave specialised trawlers available to the industry but this was not always feasible. Some of the usual fishing grounds were no longer accessible, but the trawlermen adapted and found new grounds or made use of inshore waters for the first time in many years. Despite this, there was no doubt that the fishing industry had been massively disrupted by the war but it was, albeit inadvertently, the Germans who partially solved the problem. A number of vessels from Denmark, Norway, Belgium and Holland sailed away from their invaded countries and joined the British fleet.

The families of fishermen were in a privileged position as they invariably obtained enough fish not only to feed themselves but to barter with friends and neighbours for other goods.[5] The rising price of fish, a stone of haddock had more than quadrupled in price by 1941,[6] combined with this, led to ill feeling in many fishing ports, such as North Shields in Northumberland, where many of the trawlermen had been members of the RNR and had been called up at the outbreak of war while others, who were perhaps not so patriotic, made huge profits.[7] In North Shields, boats that in pre-war years would return with catches worth perhaps £100 (£4,000 today) were instead earning up to £1,700 (£68,000 today) per trip.[8] Equitable distribution of fish was to prove a major problem throughout the war with no decent solution being discovered.[9] The queues which formed for fish (which was never rationed) were always amongst the largest and the war saw the popularity of fish and chips reach new heights as this form of fast food, once thought of as the preserve of the working class, became more socially acceptable and popular.

It was not only the deep-sea fishing industry that was affected by the war. The increasing prices of fish affected the luxury end of the market, such as salmon and sea-trout. In 1939, which was described as a 'fairly satisfactory season',[10] the price of salmon at North Shields Fish Market stood at 1s 9d per lb while that of sea-trout was 1s 6d per lb.[11] Five years later the price of salmon was 3s 5d per lb and that of sea-trout 3s 3d per lb. To make matters worse there were lesser amounts of fish being landed by the shore nets due to combinations of poor weather and the reduction in the number of men who applied for net licences. In 1939, there were forty-seven licences granted to shore nets-men in Northumberland; by 1944 this total had decreased to just eighteen.[12] Pollution, although improving, was also said to be a major factor in the paucity of catches; on more than half the days that water quality was monitored there was no detectable oxygen in the sample.[13]

Chapter 2

Dig for Victory

Growing Your Own and Rural Life in Wartime Britain

As the war had approached there had been some anxiety over the availability and price of foodstuffs in the event of war (especially amongst those who had gone through the First World War) but at Alnwick it was reported that provisions were freely available at reasonable prices (see table).

Provisions Prices at Alnwick, Northumberland, August 1939

Item	Price (average)
Eggs (per dozen)	1s 10d
Butter (per lb)	1s 3d
Flour (per stone)	1s 10d
Potatoes (per stone)	1s 3d

With many people quickly realising that the need for growing more food would be vital in this new war, a large number of those who were lucky enough to have extensive gardens patriotically sacrificed their flower beds and lawns to the plough and vegetable beds. In early October 1939 Mrs Jane H. Murray (80) agreed to plough up her beautiful lawn at her home, Dundarach, in Craiglockhart Park, Edinburgh, for the planting of potatoes and other vegetables. The lawns of Dundarach were joined in going under the plough by the grounds of Merchiston Castle Old School while part of the city's Burntisland Links were turned into allotments.

One of the first policies to have a noticeable impact upon those who lived in rural Britain was the evacuation of children and the vulnerable from many towns and cities. The evacuation of women and children from vulnerable urban areas caused significant disruption in many of the rural areas of Britain. In Northumberland, Alnwick was one of the reception areas for evacuees and was scheduled to receive and house some 1,000 people (mainly from areas of Tyneside). The first 500, consisting of schoolchildren, teachers and volunteer helpers, were due to arrive by train at Alnwick station on 1 September at 1:32 p.m. with a further 500, consisting of mothers with children under school age, following on at the same time the next day.

It seems that Alnwick had at least carried out some methodical preparation for the influx with the stations serving as a make-shift assembly centre. Well before the arrival of the train carrying evacuees emergency rations had been deposited at the station along with trestle tables and volunteers had been on duty well before the appointed time to sort the rations and erect the tables. Once disembarked the children would be organised into groups by the teachers and helpers and would take their forty-eight hours of emergency rations from their allocated tables. The emergency rations were separated into adults and children's portions. An adults' contained two tins of preserved meat, two tins of preserved milk, 1lb of biscuits, and ¼lb of chocolate. Children's carrier bags contained the same rations except they only received the one tin of preserved meat. Once they had collected their rations the groups would move towards the station's exit where they would be inspected by Dr Trevor-Roper, the Medical Officer for Health, and any cases of illness treated by a first aid party led by Mrs Collingwood Thorp which had set up its base in the general waiting room; the majority of so many wartime efforts on the home front depended upon the actions of volunteers such as Mrs Thorp and her party. After leaving the station the evacuees would be escorted to the Northumberland Hall where light refreshments were available.

From the Northumberland Hall the plan was for the evacuees to be sent to their billets as soon as possible. Alnwick had been split into twenty districts for the purposes of allocating evacuees. The council had also been in contact with those who might potentially house evacuees to reassure them that extra food supplies would be made available for their unexpected guests.

The government had plans in place for the speedy establishment of a campaign urging Britons to produce more of their own food. With the typically unimaginative and bumbling approach of the Chamberlain government the campaign had been given the uninspiring name of 'Grow More Food'. In order to encourage enough people to take part in the campaign it was recognised that the media must be brought on side. This should not have been a difficult task given that the proposed activities were healthy, would provide food and would contribute to the war effort in a meaningful way. However, given government handling of the media during this stage of the war it is little surprise that even this aim was at first thwarted.

The papers did give the launch of the campaign coverage but the ongoing events quickly overtook the rather staid message of 'Grow More Food' and the campaign quickly fell out of the headlines. Matters were not helped by sometimes mixed messages. The *National Garden Club Magazine*, for example, was cautioned for being too negative in giving its own slogan of 'Dig to Eat'.

While the Minister of Food's messages were found in the newspapers the messages relating to the campaign were generally couched in unexciting terms and did little to help newspaper editors in presenting the campaign in a positive and stimulating way. The campaign was thus hampered by an initially muddled beginning and a singularly unimaginative approach in which a lack of joined-up thinking could be seen. There were differing opinions on the campaign within the MoAg, the MoF and the Treasury. The MoAg backed the campaign but there were some who worried that amateur growers would enter into competition with farmers and market gardeners, while some within the MoF had similar worries that amateur producers would reduce the profits of food retailers.

It largely fell to the press to provide a replacement slogan which more effectively captured the public imagination. In 1939, Michael Foot was a leader writer for the *Evening Standard*. Noted for his fiery left-wing rhetoric he was one of those who can be credited for the bold headline in the newspaper on 6 September 1939. The article launched the newspaper's own campaign for the British public to do their bit in the garden (before the government got around to launching Grow More Food) but did so using the simple headline 'DIG'. Six days later the newspaper ran an editorial which exhorted the British people to 'Dig for Victory'. Foot's inspiration was not credited to him until his obituary was published in 2010. The reasons for this are not known but it is possible that Foot saw in the Dig for Victory slogan a socialist campaign in which the masses would return to the land. Whatever the reasons, the encouraging slogan caught the public imagination and was quickly adopted. It told people they were contributing to the war effort and that the war effort would be successful.

Those within the campaign initially were hugely hampered by wastefulness and an overly thrifty approach from the Treasury. The campaign got off to a very poor start and by the early weeks of 1940 questions were being asked. In a parliamentary debate in February the former Prime Minister, David Lloyd George, attacked the campaign stating that all gardeners were being urged to get behind this grand scheme and had been promised that the government would provide fertiliser yet it had become known that a limit for these fertilisers had been set at just £1,000. Attacking the policy, Lloyd George concluded that the campaign was being seriously damaged by such penny-pinching measures and that 'You cannot dig for victory with a pair of Treasury scissors'.

Despite a growing commitment amongst sections of the British public it was not until 1941 that the Dig for Victory campaign really took off. Shortages were now biting very deeply and it had become clear that with farmers being instructed to grow specific crops such as barley, wheat, potatoes, and feed for animals there would be further shortages of some hitherto common vegetables such as beans, carrots and cabbages. With the introduction of double-summer time people were encouraged to use every available hour of daylight to grow their own vegetables, to Dig for Victory.

Much of the onus at the time was placed upon women. Growing their own vegetables, they were told, was their duty, not only as a member of the British public during wartime but as mothers. The best way to ensure that their children grew up with a healthy diet was to ensure that sufficient vegetables were grown and eaten. Those without gardens were exhorted to go to their local council and ask for an allotment plot. The number of plots available had been massively increased but there were still many families who would not be able to obtain a plot of their own and many resorted to sharing plots with neighbours or extended family members.

We have seen how the MoF under Woolton and, to a lesser extent, the MoAg under Hudson were increasingly willing to fund huge propaganda campaigns. The Dig for Victory campaign was at the forefront of this effort. Numerous leaflets were published and widely disseminated. They formed the basis of a course on smallholding for those who had never grown their own food before. The advice offered in the leaflets was generally very useful, but it did tend to make assumptions. Most of the published materials, for example, tended to assume that people had access to quite large plots of land. Typically, a plot resembling an allotment plot of 30'x90' was assumed. This was fine for allotment holders but there were few fortunate enough to own houses with gardens of a comparable size. Nevertheless, the advice offered proved extremely valuable throughout the war and did enable many people to grow a sufficiency of vegetables for their own needs.

The success of the Dig for Victory campaign led to many enthusiastic gardeners realising that they could be more successful if they combined their efforts and, as a result, locally organised groups and associations sprang up across the country. In rural areas, where more growing space was readily available, many of these groups realised they could make a significant contribution to the war effort.

In Gloucestershire in 1941, a leading member of the Home Food Production Club in Ebley realised that planting individual potato crops in their gardens was wasteful and an unproductive effort compared to what might be possible if they combined their efforts. A motion was thus passed which established a potato co-operative which would seek to plant an acre of potatoes (and thus qualify for a government payment). It was agreed that initial membership would cost 5s and would be open to forty people but so popular did the scheme prove that it became over-subscribed and some people were even turned away.

After a suitable piece of ground had been identified the co-operative set to work. The labour, when shared in such a manner, proved to be far easier with it being estimated that, harvesting aside, each member spent only eight to ten hours working on the plot. By the end of the project each member had paid the sum of 10s 6d, but for this they received between 6 and 7 hundredweight of potatoes.

The co-operative scheme was such a success that a BBC edition of *Back to the Land* highlighted the scheme in October 1942 and the scheme was later used as a plan for such cooperatives in other parts of rural Britain.

The highly successful Dig for Victory campaigns saw millions growing vegetables for the first time in their lives. For others, the growing of vegetables for home consumption was nothing new. In Northumberland many people, especially those in poorer paid jobs, were well used to the practice and many leek clubs and horticultural societies already existed before the war. One way in which morale could be maintained alongside the growing of food was in the annual shows of produce which took place across the country but which were especially popular in places such as Northumberland. In August 1943 the Berwick & District Horticultural Society held its show in Tweedmouth. The proceeds of the event, mainly raised through refreshments and the sale of the produce, was donated to the Red Cross.

With the vast majority of the public solidly behind the national war effort the government was determined to further encourage people to become involved through making the most of their food supplies and through digging for victory. One of the four mobile projection units which it had in Scotland was based in Edinburgh and during the city's Food Week the unit showed sixty-nine public film shows to a variety of groups including clubs, the WVS, works canteens, schools, Church organisations, Co-operative Guilds, and Women's Guilds.

People who were digging for victory were offered valuable assistance through official and unofficial channels. The press across Britain regularly published columns which gave useful gardening advice to amateurs. On Orkney the column gave hints and tips on the growing of vegetables but also on the rearing of stock such as pigs and poultry. One of the most popular and long-running columns in the *Orkney Herald* was 'Vegetables for Victory' by George E. Greenhowe of the North of Scotland College for Agriculture. One of his typical columns provided hints on the sowing of early carrots, giving instructions on how to sow the carrots and also advice on which varieties were best suited. The column also advised that cauliflowers and Brussels sprouts which had been grown on in cold frames could now be planted out. Mr Greenhowe also advised on how a small sowing of early Milan turnips could be sowed between rows of broad beans or rows marked out for sprouts. He also cautioned that it would be beneficial to plant more leeks this year than had been the norm so that adequate supplies would be available in winter and the spring of 1944.

With food shortages and supplies still at severe risk Orcadians were repeatedly encouraged to try to grow as much of their own food as possible. A series of campaigns were launched to further this aim, the most famous, of course, being Dig for Victory. The Scottish Gardens and Allotments Committee, the Department of Agriculture for Scotland, the Ministry of Food and the Scottish Women's Voluntary Institute (SWVI), maintained a van which toured the country manned by an expert on vegetable gardening and a qualified cook and nutritionist. The van had been in use for several years but had never crossed to Orkney until May 1944. The van was specially equipped but when it arrived at Kirkwall the weather was very poor and the demonstrations had to be relocated to the Grammar School. Miss Harrison, the gardening expert, gave a very practical talk on the growing of vegetables and urged all to grow more of these valuable foods. She also introduced a wartime film which described how vegetables and the gardener were on the front lines in this war. Cook and nutritionist, Miss Gillies gave a very good demonstration of vegetable cooking techniques and showed a film on fruit bottling. Both women afterwards answered a series of questions posed by the large audience.

The 'Vegetables for Victory' column in May 1944 described, amongst other tips and hints, how to use and prepare liquid manure. This, he wrote, must always be diluted to the appearance of weak tea and when being applied should not touch the foliage. While the most effective manure came from the farm manure heap, when this was not available it was perfectly feasible to make one's own. To do this, advised the column, take a bucketful of cow manure or sheep droppings and suspend them, enclosed in a close mesh sack, in a large vessel containing rain-water for a few days. Guano could also be employed as a liquid manure by dissolving 3oz in 10 gallons of water.

The changing circumstances in the countryside led to several unforeseen problems as vermin populations now became a far more bitter enemy and there were fewer people available to maintain control over these populations. Game was also a matter for concern. One consequence of the war, and in particular the labour shortage, was that the control of the deer population became an increasing problem. As a result, deer were culled in large numbers with venison, which was unrationed, becoming more available on the market. Some butchers were fortunate enough to be able to cash in on this windfall. In Ross & Cromarty, Dingwall butcher Murdo McGregor was one such man. Mr McGregor would appear to have had a contract to dispose of much of the venison produced as a result of the culling and over the festive season in 1940–1941 he was advertising venison in large quantities. Such were the profits of the enterprising butcher that later in 1941 he was able to buy out a Dingwall High Street rival, was selling wholesale and had opened up a branch in Strathpeffer.

The deer shooting season which ended in October 1941 had been badly affected by the severity of the late winter weather which caused a great many deer to die in the large snowdrifts (some of which were 30 feet deep). The numbers of deer culled was also affected by the shortage of rifles, keepers and ghillies. Despite these problems, the season was adjudged a successful one but, although many hundredweights of venison had been sent to canning factories and cold storage, the sum was not half of that of the previous year. The manager of one canning factory complained that he had only received 10 per cent of the venison compared to the previous two years and the quality of the venison was not of the same standard of 1939–1940. Stalkers concurred with this view, reporting that stags were underweight and in poor condition compared to previous years. Keepers and ghillies at Glenquoich reported that stags were 1½ stone lighter than average. This was put down to the severe weather conditions. Other reasons were also put forward. One vastly experienced Inverness-shire stalker blamed the increase in hand-feeding of stags which, he said, had led to the beasts becoming unused to fending for themselves in harsh weather. A neighbouring stalker blamed the cull of the previous year stating that too many deer had been culled and that tenants and proprietors should be more cautious as over-culling of the deer would have massive ramifications at the end of the war when many keepers and ghillies who were away with the forces would find themselves out of work.

Much of the venison brought down from the hills went to be processed but many landowners, keen to be seen to do their patriotic duty, made extensive donations of the meat produced on their land. Amongst these donors were the King and Queen. Following a visit to Balmoral the King offered royal venison to the communal feeding centres all over Scotland. One of the first to benefit from this magnanimous gesture was the feeding centre at Leith. Royal venison was also sent to various schools. At the beginning of October, for example, Balmoral venison was sent to the school meal services of Dundee Education Committee. These donations were widely publicised. In September 1941 *The Scotsman* reported that royal venison, at least six haunches, had been sent to Edinburgh. Some of the venison was served at the opening of The Laden Creel, North Fort Street, Leith. This was the sixth communal feeding centre in the city and the third in the port of Leith. Others who contributed venison at this time included Mr C.M. Rose of Rhidorroch, Ross-shire; Marquess of Zetland, Letterewe, Ross-shire; Colonel MacKenzie, Farr, Inverness-shire; Major Stirling, Fairburn, Ross-shire; Major A. H. Wilkie, Corrie Laid, Glenmoriston; Captain E. C. Clarke, Fasnakyle; the Cojlin Estate, Kinlochewe, Ross-shire; Seafield Estate, Balmacaan; Inverness-shire; Lovat Estate, Beauly, Inverness-shire; and Glenmoriston Estate.

We have previously encountered the entrepreneurship of Dingwall butcher, Murdo McGregor, who had cashed in on the venison boom of 1939–1940. As we have also seen, however, the largesse did not last and by the Christmas of 1943 Mr McGregor could only advertise venison as poor quality and with an irregular supply. The enterprising butcher, however, did find another way. At the same time as his venison supplies collapsed he was able to advertise prime quality geese and ducks; again, produce which was off ration.

The war entered into the country-dwellers' life in unexpected ways. We have already seen how farmers had to give up their land in order to allow the construction of airfields and defences. The war also intervened in other ways, from the presence of servicemen and women in previously quiet villages and market towns to the dropping of stray bombs through to the horrific scenes which followed the crash of an aircraft.

With the growing number of aircraft sorties being made by Allied bombers came an increase in the number of crashes when stricken bombers failed to make it back to their airfield. Many times the aircraft crashed on farmland and farmers and agricultural workers were often the first on the scene to these frightful scenes. Shortly before midnight on 15/16 January 1943 a Vickers Wellington IC (Z1078) of 150 Squadron was attempting to return to its home airfield at Snaith in Yorkshire from a mission to Hamburg when it ran into difficulties. The aircraft was in navigational difficulties and its radio equipment was unserviceable. The aircraft wandered north over the Northumbrian Cheviot Hills in snow and heavy mist and, not realising they were over high ground, the pilot crashed into West Hill on Cheviot itself.

This extremely remote area was very sparsely populated but local shepherds realised an aircraft had crashed when they smelled burning and John Dagg and two friends set off up the hill with Mr Dagg's sheepdog Sheila. We shall meet Sheila and Mr Dagg later. When they reached the crash site one of the six-man crew was already dead and the others were injured. The three shepherds extricated the survivors and managed to alert the authorities; sadly, of the initial survivors two later succumbed to their injuries.

On the night of 15 October two more Northumbrian shepherds found themselves confronted by a crashed bomber. The Halifax bomber (DK116) was on a training flight from 1667 Heavy Conversion Unit but crashed in the isolated country around Kielder. The bomber suffered an engine fire and the pilot ordered the crew to bail out. Three did so but the rear gunner became trapped in his turret and, while the remaining two crew fought to release him, the pilot desperately put the bomber into a steep dive in the hope that it would put out the fire. Unfortunately, the bomber crashed into high ground at Caplestone Fell on Glendhu Hill, killing the four crew instantly. Adam Steele of Willow Bog Farm had been visiting a fellow shepherd at nearby High Long House and the two men were walking back to Mr Steele's house when they witnessed the crash. Despite the darkness and the rough terrain, the two shepherds immediately set off to see if there were any survivors. They discovered the dead crewmen and also located two of the survivors, one of whom was suffering from a broken leg. The shepherds comforted the shocked airmen until more locals arrived and they were able to evacuate the survivors to waiting ambulances some 5 miles away.

Almost three years after Northumbrian shepherd John Dagg had played a key role in the rescue of several RAF aircrew from a crashed bomber he once again found himself confronted with a crashed bomber. On 16 December 1944, the 303rd Bomb Group (Heavy) of the United States Army Air Force (USAAF) had aborted an attack on the marshalling yards at Ulm due to bad weather, but one B-17G (44-6504) became hopelessly lost upon return and drifted over Northumberland. The bomber, still with a full bombload aboard, descended to try to establish its location but crashed onto West Hill on the Cheviot. Two of the nine men aboard were killed and the others injured as the wreckage skidded, disintegrating as it went, across a peat bog.

John Dagg and another shepherd, Frank Moscrop, realised that an aircraft had crashed. They quickly organised a search party of nine locals but held little hope of locating the crash in the blizzard which was blowing at the time. The best hope for finding the site was Mr Dagg's dog, Sheila. Sure enough, Sheila discovered the survivors hours later. Sheila, Mr Dagg and Mr Moscrop then led the survivors down the hill to Mr Dagg's cottage where they could await transport. The rescue attracted world-wide attention with extensive coverage of the event in the US press. The *Chicago Tribune* related the details of the story and paid especial tribute to the 60-year-old shepherd (Mr Dagg) who had formed the rescue party and then led the way as they took part in an arduous and lengthy climb up the steep mountain while the storm raged unabated. It was largely the tenacity combined with local knowledge which allowed them to succeed.

We have already seen how farmers received praise for their efforts in ploughing up their land in order to produce more arable crops. It was not only farmers who received such praise. In an effort to maintain the momentum of the various Dig for Victory campaigns those who struggled to produce food in allotments, gardens and on waste ground came in for widespread praise. The government was keenly aware of how vital the contribution of private citizens was and was also aware that the growing of food on allotments and in gardens was a boost to morale as it meant that people felt involved in the war effort.

The V-Weapon attacks which began in 1944 led to several parts of northern England once again receiving evacuees. This time the evacuees came from the south, especially the London area. Northumberland once again welcomed these newcomers despite the fact that billets were scarce. The local press fronted a campaign to house the evacuees. The evacuees were sorted into three distinct groups: unaccompanied schoolchildren; mothers with infant children; and expecting or nursing mothers. Once again, the evacuees were encouraged to play a full role in their adopted communities and newspaper coverage of young evacuees throwing themselves into rural life were commonplace in the communities which welcomed this new wave of evacuees.

Criminal Exploitation

While the vast majority of those who took part in the production of their own foods followed the guidelines which the government placed upon such activities, others fell afoul of the myriad restrictions. Often, these unfortunate folk were simply the victims of ignorance or an unfortunate oversight but others deliberately undertook such criminal endeavours.

The scarcity of food drove some to criminal activities, even during the crisis year of 1940. In Northumberland cases of hoarding were rare but here, as across Britain, there were those who made substantial use of the black market. Although this was illegal and, in some cases, could be immoral the majority of such criminal activity was in the form of provisioners providing 'extras' to customers. Others found elicit food supplies in more traditional ways.

The River Coquet at Rothbury had been a traditional haunt of smugglers in the nineteenth century and this tradition was revived by some who were short of food or sensed an opportunity for profit. In November Mr John Shell of Pine Tree House, Rothbury, was arrested for using a gaff to illegally fish for salmon at Thrum Mill, Rothbury. Mr Shell was apprehended by a water bailiff after he was observed gaffing and killing a salmon. Upon arrest Mr Shell had thrown his walking stick and attached gaff into the river in an effort to dispose of some of the evidence but had admitted gaffing the fish. The bailiffs later recovered the gaff and Mr Shell had little option but to plead guilty to the charges proffered against him. While trying to explain his actions Mr Shell stated that his wife liked the taste of salmon and that he acted only to obtain food as rations were 'very scarce just now [but there were] any amount of fish so I thought I would have a bit of fish. I thought there was no harm in having a bit of fish when so many were going past.' The bench were unimpressed by this excuse and fined Mr Shell the sum of £1 2s 6d.

Despite the determination to contribute to the war effort, highlighted by the popularity of pig clubs, there were still cases of people avoiding new regulations appearing before the courts on Orkney. On 19 August 1941, while the local War Weapons Week was in full swing, three such cases, all of them linked, were heard by Sheriff Brown at Kirkwall. Mr John George Stanger had allegedly fallen afoul of the Livestock (Restriction on Slaughtering) Order, 1940, being accused of, by the hands of two of his employees, having caused a pig to be slaughtered without possessing a licence from the Ministry of Food. Mr James Flett, representing Mr Stanger, told the court that Mr Stanger pleaded guilty to the charge but that he had merely followed his practice of 50 years and he had no idea that he had done wrong. Ignorance of the law, of course, is no defence and the Fiscal replied that he could not believe an experienced farmer such as Mr Stanger, who farmed on a fairly large scale, could be unaware of the regulations which had been in force for some time now and that if this was allowed to pass then other farmers would use it to get around rationing regulations. Mr Flett once again stated that his client had acted only in accordance with long-established tradition on his farm, that he was unaware of the regulation and pleaded with the court to show leniency for what was a first offence. Sheriff Brown was not moved by this argument and stated that he could not accept that Mr Stanger was ignorant of the law regarding the slaughtering of livestock for human consumption. He therefore imposed a fine of £5 upon Mr Stanger with the alternative of 30 days' imprisonment.

The second part of the case involved a Dounby merchant, Mr James Oag, who was charged with being in possession of the carcass of the above pig without a licence. It was illegal for anyone without a licence to have in their possession, sell, expose for sale or otherwise dispose of such a carcass. Solicitor William Davis stated that his client knew nothing of the order in question and that this was a mere technical breach of the order and that the accused had no profit from having the carcass in his possession. He therefore suggested that a suitable punishment would be a simple admonishment. The sheriff said that he would defer sentencing until he had heard the final part of the case.

The final part of the case of the pig that did not go to market involved another merchant. John George Jolly of Harray was accused of producing 134lbs of bacon from a carcass without possession of the necessary licence contrary to the Bacon (Licensing of Producers) Order, 1939. Representing Mr Jolly, Mr C.E.S. Wallis tendered a guilty plea. The Fiscal told Sheriff Brown that Ministry of Food employees had entered a shed on Mr Jolly's premises and found five pieces of pork in the course of being turned into bacon. Four of these were traced back to the pig mentioned above and it was noted that Mr Jolly's initial claim that he had bought the meat ordinarily and was preparing to pickle it to preserve it was proven false by the lack of string marks on the bacon. Mr Jolly, the sheriff was told, did not have a licence to produce bacon to which Mr Wallis stated that his client was a licensed dealer in meat and that he had only agreed to cure the pork which had been brought to him by Mr Oag so as to prevent it going bad. Mr Jolly also stated that, in his opinion, it would have been better to sell the carcass as fresh pork.

Sheriff Brown sentenced both Mr Oag and Mr Jolly to pay £5 or face 30 days' imprisonment and in summing up the case said that he believed it represented a scheme to avoid the rationing regulation and was thus a very serious matter. He added that any further such cases brought before him would be more harshly punished. Indeed, Sheriff Brown had been lenient as the possible punishment for such offences included a fine of up to £100, three months' imprisonment, or both.

Allotments

Relying on the traditional English passion for gardening, the Dig for Victory campaign, backed by huge spending on propaganda by the MoF, was a massive success. The MoF's backing for the campaign did not flag throughout the war. In 1942 the MoF distributed some 10,000,000 leaflets instructing people how to grow various foodstuffs or look after livestock such as pigs or poultry. While the possibility of turning the garden over to food production was an attractive one it could only apply to those who had a garden. Many, especially those living in towns and cities, did not. Allotments were one answer. In 1939 there were 815,000 allotment plots in Britain but by 1943 this number had increased to 1,400,000 and many manual workers threw themselves into working their own plot. By the end of the war more than half of all such workers reported that they were keeping an allotment or a garden.

In common with most other areas, the Dig for Victory campaign enjoyed widespread popularity on Wearside with many householders replacing flower gardens with crops, taking on allotments or joining pig or poultry clubs. In 1941 the Royal Horticultural Society and the Ministry of Agriculture had put on a very successful display of photographs of vegetables at Sunderland Museum. This success was followed in July 1942 with an exhibition which concentrated on the pests which afflicted vegetable gardeners. The exhibition, held in the conveniently titled Gardeners' Friends and Foes section of the museum, included depictions and descriptions of pests such as wire worm, cut worm, gall weevil, carrot, cabbage and onion flies, the flea beetle, the millipede and centipede as well as advice on how to best combat the pests.

The Dig for Victory campaign continued apace all year round with gardeners, allotment holders, pig and chicken clubs all being exhorted to even greater efforts. At Portobello, Edinburgh, a meeting was addressed by the secretary of the Scottish Gardens and Allotments Committee, Mr George F. Porthouse, who told them that 'More people are growing vegetables in Scotland than ever before' and that the number of allotments had increased fourfold since the war began with over 80,000 allotments now being tended in Scotland. More than ever people were also growing vegetables in their own gardens and this was to be praised but Mr Porthouse also warned that the next winter and the spring of 1944 would, he thought, be the most testing period yet faced and so plans had to be put in place immediately and the growing of winter and storage crops had to be greatly increased. As vegetable supplies from England would not be so easily obtainable it was essential that Scotland increase her own production and 'make a supreme effort to attain self-sufficiency'. In order to accomplish this as the tempo of the war increased still further, Mr Porthouse said, 'the kitchen plot would assume still greater importance'.[1]

One result of the Dig for Victory campaign was a huge upswing in interest in allotments. For those who did not have access to a garden the possibility of an allotment meant that they too could make a contribution by growing their own food. Allotments sprung up in all manner of unlikely locations with bomb-sites proving particularly popular in areas which had been victim of enemy action. One of the greatest success stories was that of the Bethnal Green Bombed Sites Association (BGSA). The neighbourhood was one of the most heavily bombed in Britain and suffered at least 3,200 houses destroyed or left in a ruinous state. The association sprang from a meeting held on 24 April 1942. The meeting was to consider what use could be made of the numerous bombed and cleared sites in the area with a view to providing amenities and increasing the growth of food. The meeting was capitalising on a previous initiative in the previous year which had led, for example, to the local residents digging up the concrete playground of a bombed school in order to grow vegetables.

As a result of the meeting, it was decided to form an association which would support the large numbers of local residents who wished to grow their own vegetables but who were largely prevented from doing so thanks to a lack of gardens at their cramped residences. There had already been considerable interest shown locally in established allotment sites with the nearby Victoria Park site being almost at full capacity. Therefore, it was felt that this association might secure more sites for the use of residents. The association adopted the motto 'Quality and not Quantity' and also agreed on three main aims which were to negotiate for the rights to suitable sites, to promote the interests of members and to provide guidance and instruction to its members.

By the end of June the association had successfully identified thirty-two possible sites and was involved in negotiations to secure them. Early boosts to the cause came from the Metropolitan Gardens Association which promised to send a horticultural expert to advise the newly formed association and from Oxford House and the WVS who both donated some simple gardening equipment.

By 1943 the association was successfully overseeing the management of over 300 allotments spread over more than 10 acres of land. Plots had a wide variance in size with the largest being 2,000 yards square. A children's allotment was set up at Russia Lane and a model allotment was established at Ravenscroft Street in which new members were given training. Membership at the time stood at over 400 and, in addition to vegetable production, the members were also rearing more than 6,000 animals, many of which were housed in especially constructed housing. In the constricted space rabbits were the most popular type of livestock, making up 4,000 of the total. They were followed by 2,000 chickens while smaller numbers of pigs, goats, ducks and geese were also reared.

With many of the sites being heavily littered with rubble and other heavy items of debris the BGSA called often upon the expertise of the War Debris Survey Department which was run by London County Council and the various organisations built up an impressive rate of collaboration.

For such organisations money was always a concern but the enthusiasm and patriotic spirit of the time, enhanced by the popularity of the Dig for Victory campaign, ensured that support was often forthcoming. Fully aware of the financial penury of many residents the BGSA charged an initial fee of just 1s (this was raised in 1943 to 2s) but benefited from monetary donations from a variety of sources. Amongst the greatest support was that which came from John Percy Mitchelhill, a theatrical entrepreneur. Mitchelhill had already turned over the gardens of his home for the blind in Kentish Town to Dig for Victory participants and the BGSA was naturally of interest to him. In addition to monetary donations he also provided the association with over 400 items of gardening equipment while the Mitchelhill Cup was the prize awarded to BGSA's best allotment competition. Regular donations also came from as far afield as Brazil, from someone who had heard about the BGSA in a radio broadcast. On a more mundane, but no less useful, level the local council agreed to donate the manure heap which lay in the Ion Square Gardens.

One of the early donations had been set aside to allow the recruitment of a technical adviser but this was one of the areas in which the association's leadership struggled. Several candidates dropped out at the last minute and this forced the association to increase the funding available for the post before, finally, a Miss King was secured at a weekly salary of £4 10s. The tenure of Miss King was not a success and there were several complaints about her performance. This led to an inquiry in the summer of 1943 and although there was no evidence found of any specific wrongdoing on the part of Miss King the committee did agree that the technical adviser had at times been careless in her use of funds and she moved on just weeks later to another position.

Other problems experienced by the BGSA were those experienced by many participants in Dig for Victory. Pilfering was a persistent problem in some areas but was usually of a relatively minor nature although it could be heartbreaking to the gardener who went to his or her plot only to find that hours, days and even weeks of hard work had been wasted by some thoughtless person. Children and youths were often blamed for these crimes but efforts to crack down on them largely proved fruitless. In the summer of 1942, for example, the BGSA was reporting that the children's allotment at 57/65 Russia Lane had been experiencing a great deal of difficulty due to theft and vandalism.

Despite these difficulties the BGSA was a huge success but was one which was recognised as being largely a wartime only creation which would not last long in times of peace and, indeed, it was acknowledged that perhaps only fifty plots might be tenable in peacetime.

Pig and Poultry Clubs

While Dig for Victory attracted the most attention it was by no means the only way in which the British public produced their own food. Those with access to allotments or other larger spaces could rear pigs, poultry or rabbits and even where space was confined clubs quickly formed for similar reasons.

Small pig clubs grew rapidly during the war. Typical of these was the Warkworth and District Pig Club in Northumberland which formed in May 1943 under the chairmanship of a local councillor. Demonstrating the usefulness of the War Ags, the inaugural address and lecture was delivered by the regional officers of the Small Pig Keepers Council. The subject was the management of pig clubs and the advantages of the forming and running of such clubs. A second speaker gave a lecture on the mysteries of pig feeding and the use of differing foodstuffs in producing pigs.

In rural Britain it was not only farming on a large scale which provided foodstuffs. Smallholders and those who endeavoured to grow their own food in gardens and whatever space could be found were commonplace in most areas. During the war this spread to the towns and cities. Up until the summer of 1940 most town-dwellers had been prevented from keeping livestock or poultry by governmental restrictions. After these restrictions were lifted the government, assisted by groups such as the RSPCA, produced numerous leaflets encouraging the keeping of a few animals where possible and giving advice as to how the animals could be cared for. The idea of keeping one's own animals quickly appealed and private individuals and clubs quickly set about obtaining their own beasts.

The keeping of hens was already commonplace in many rural areas but with the shortages of eggs and the fact that poultry meat was off-ration the keeping of a few hens appealed to many town-dwellers too. Across Britain people began cobbling together henhouses out of whatever wood or other materials they could find or scavenge. The amateur poultry keeper was kept from entering into competition with the established market through restrictions which meant that no more than twenty-five hens could be kept. If more than this were kept the keeper had to register as a commercial poultry keeper and his/her eggs had to be sold to a packing station where they entered the formal rationing system. Feeding the poultry was accomplished through the feeding of kitchen scraps but many also took advantage of the offer to trade in their tiny fresh egg ration allocation for access to poultry meal. It quickly became obvious to many that greater success could be had through co-operation with friends, family or neighbours and poultry clubs were the next logical step.

Eggs became increasingly scarce and, with many people disliking the dried egg which was on offer, from the summer of 1941 people were rationed to one egg per week. People were warned, however, that this would go down to one per fortnight in the winter months. The demand for eggs sometimes reached fever pitch and many people, encouraged by the MoF, began keeping hens either in their own gardens as a private venture, on allotments or as part of a poultry club. So precious were fresh eggs that various ingenious solutions were carried out to preserve them in times of plenty. Smearing the shells with a dry preservative sealed them, as did submerging them in waterglass (made from the swim bladders of fish).

Another option for many families was to keep rabbits. This was a less profitable enterprise than poultry keeping but required less space. Amateurs were confined to the keeping of no more than eight rabbits or be registered as a professional breeder. Unlike the case of poultry, however, a professional breeder, while forced to sell their meat or rabbits officially, could sell to who they wished.

For the amateur enthused by the Dig for Victory campaign, advice was offered on the growing of vegetables but also on raising livestock where possible. Hens and rabbits were immensely popular but so were pigs and pig clubs sprang up in every town and village in Northumberland. In 1941 an article in the *Morpeth Herald* concluded with some advice to those who had started keeping a pig or two. Research at an agricultural college had revealed that pigs could be successfully reared on a mix of meal with young grass clippings from the lawn (although care had to be taken not to give them too much grass). The writer, under the pen-name Agricola, advised that a normal rate of growth could be maintained by adding such lawn clippings (as a wet slop mixed with meal) to a daily allowance of no more than 2½lb per pig.

Perhaps the most popular species to raise, however, proved to be the pig. Easily fed on scraps from the kitchen, from ingredients that could be collected in the wild or, where there was space, foraging for food themselves the pig could provide a family with a glut of meat and other products. Swill could be obtained from local councils who collected food waste and boiled it down to sell on. In no case was the club mentality seen more obviously than in the formation of pig clubs. So successful did these become that the demand for pig meal grew to huge proportions and the MoF was forced to cut the amount available in 1942. Undeterred the pig clubs found alternative sources of food. Indeed, pig clubs became such a popular wartime phenomena that by the end of the wear there were almost 7,000 clubs registered across the country.

The pig club idea was not a new one. It was, in fact, an idea resurrected from the First World War but this conflict saw it embraced on a far larger scale. The pig clubs allowed people to not only contribute to the war effort while feeding themselves and their friends, they also fulfilled a special role in maintaining morale. By October 1940 there were 200 clubs registered with the Small Pig Keepers' Council (who were responsible for keeping the records of the various pig clubs). The honour of becoming the two hundredth club demonstrated the variety of people who were organising themselves into clubs. The honour was taken by the London Zookeepers Pig Club. The keepers purchased ten pigs and, like many clubs, had constructed their own sties and pighouses out of material which was otherwise going to waste. The opening of the club was attended by the MP for Honiton, Mr Cedric Drewe. By August 1942 the pig club had grown and, with the original inhabitants being sent elsewhere, the pigs had taken over the warthog enclosure.

The pig club at London Zoo was only one effort which was put in place at the zoo. In August of 1942 an exhibition was put on which instructed people in the skills needed to keep animals for food production at home. In addition to the pig club mentioned above the zoo had also made some changes itself. The reptile house had been taken over by rabbits, while the land beside the parrot house had been given over to some 500 hens. The zoo had also turned over some of its research activities to considering how to prevent insect despoliation of food crops.

The sheer variety of clubs is astounding. They ranged from sections of Home Guard, local corporation workers, miners, football and other sports club members, workers on noble estates, to the police; all created pig clubs. They ranged in size from those with just a handful of members to grander affairs where committees oversaw their actions and significant contributions were made not only to supplying members but also to supplying the MoF. At the beginning of February 1942, for example, the *Gloucester Journal* covered one of these larger pig clubs. It was formed from the men of the Cleansing Department of Gloucester Corporation and consisted of forty-three members who each held an equal share and was overseen by an elected committee (the Cleansing Superintendent was Secretary and Treasurer). The objectives of the newly established club were threefold. To provide food for members and their families, to provide food for the nation, and to encourage members to save more household waste.

The police forces around Britain seem to have been particularly keen organisers and members of pig clubs. In London, the first police pig club had been formed by officers at the Union Grove station. It had been so successful that it had sponsored and aided the foundation of a further eight clubs and by 1941 it had outgrown its quarters. Land was at a premium, but the police managed to secure the spacious site at the Notre Dame Convent on Clapham Common. By August of that year the club, under the eye of its technical adviser, PC Newnham, and its secretary, PC Dipper, had relocated there. The eight-acre site became the centre of a large-scale effort by the police and, in addition to the pig club, housed 155 allotment plots (with plans for more). PC Newnham and PC Dipper's efforts with the pig club were so successful that it was using just 1½cwt of its 15cwt monthly pig meal allowance and was thus saving valuable pig meal in addition to providing food. The profits from the pig club were donated to the War Savings Committee and the very first such donation had been £54. One of the inspirations behind the success of the site was the enthusiasm and support of the Clapham sub-division senior officer, Inspector Bartlett. The success of the Notre Dame Convent site was such that in the summer of 1941 it received a visit from the Minister of Agriculture, accompanied by the Commissioner of Police, Sir Philip Game, and other senior officers from elsewhere in the capital.

With the growing shortages the popularity of pig clubs spread throughout the land. In the capital numerous groups got together. We have already seen how the police began their own rather grand scheme. It was not only the authorities which encouraged the pig clubs, even Harrods got in on the act. The up-market store set up its own piggery display using pigs loaned from the Hyde Park Pig Club in order to demonstrate how to care not only for pigs but also for poultry and rabbits (all of which the club raised).

One problem facing the new owners of pigs was that the majority of them knew nothing of butchering livestock. To counter this the MoF and other concerned groups toured Britain visiting pig clubs to give demonstrations on butchery. These gave instruction on the preserving of the meat but also, one of the key appeals of the pig, demonstrated how almost every part of the carcass and its by-products could be utilised. Sausages were, of course, obvious but other suggestions included the making of black pudding, brawn, faggots and, of course, pork pies.

The availability of meat from pigs attracted black-market opportunities. One Shropshire farmer was caught storing pork down a well in order to avoid detection. Others secretly distributed joints of meat using delivery vans or through more devious means such as using prams. There were allegations that in many rural areas the local police often turned a blind eye to these activities so long as they remained largely small in nature. Many rural police officers were themselves customers and most police forces also had their own, legal, pig clubs.

As we have seen, pig rearing, in particular, became hugely popular with those with gardens or allotments, as well as farmers and smallholders, eagerly acquiring pigs. The government viewed this positively with anyone being allowed to keep a pig so long as they also kept another which was reared at the same time but which was donated to the MoF for national use. Abuses of the system were rife with many obtaining a third pig which would be slaughtered for their own use. Pigs were attractive for several reasons. They could be fed on scraps which had been suitably prepared as well as rooting for their own sustenance. The meat from the pig could be used in a variety of ways. As well as joints of pork the meat could be turned into sausages, bacon, ham, brawn could be made from head meat and other offal while the blood could be used to make black pudding. Hams and sides of bacon would be cured, hung in sheds, cellars or lofts while some went so far as to bury a half-pig in a bath of salt.

Pigs also served in another way by reducing the wastage of food. Professional merchants quickly got in on the act with one, Silcocks, launching an advertising campaign stating that beating food waste also beat the U-Boats. The government introduced regulations which stated that all rejected food had to be processed by companies which were authorised to process it and produce swill. In the urban areas of Britain swill tubs and bins appeared on street corners, chained to lamp-posts, with locals asked to contribute potato peelings and other suitable food waste. Local councils used the collected waste to produce swill in especially installed and sometimes adapted plants. Cheltenham Corporation, for example, utilised three old tar boilers to produce 50 tons of high-quality swill every month. Tottenham had been the first local authority to build a plant to produce such food and, thus, the product, which could be fed to either pigs or poultry, became known as Tottenham Pudding.

Pig clubs were extensively encouraged and enthusiastically taken up by various people, groups and organisations up and down the country. In Scotland, community pig clubs proved to be massively popular with over 900 being officially set up. Schools also got in on the act with the resulting joints and pork products being sold off to the parents of pupils.

In rural areas it was even easier to obtain food for pigs. Acorns and beech mast were commonly used and the MoAg even instructed farmers to come to agreements with local schools for children to collect acorns for pig feed, claiming that dried acorns were highly nutritious.

In many towns and cities pig bins were placed upon street corners and residents were encouraged to deposit their kitchen scraps in them. Official publicity informed the public that the scraps from fifteen typical houses was suitable to feed one pig, after the scraps had been mixed with a small amount of meal. In many towns and cities the bins were regularly emptied (Watford received particular praise for its efficiency) but there were complaints from other areas in which unemptied bins began to stink. There were also some stories of people placing glass and other unsuitable material in the bins but these incidents were in fact relatively rare and the bins were largely a success.

The pig clubs which were quickly formed tended to be of two distinct types. The first type consisted of groups where individual members raised their own animals. Such individuals could have two pigs per year slaughtered and while most meat was used either by the owner or shared amongst the club members it was allowable to sell up to a full side of meat to a local butcher, but at a wholesale price. The second type of pig club had members acting as a co-operative to rear animals. Members of this type of club were restricted to claiming only half of the meat which they produced but were to sell the remainder to retailers which were on a government-approved list. It would seem, however, that far from the commonplace of using everything but the oink, both groups sold on a majority of their meat. It was found that individual rearers sold on 62 per cent of their meat while for the cooperatives the total was just 10 per cent higher.

The dustmen of Tottenham quickly realised that their profession allowed them access to a large amount of suitable feed on a daily basis. After receiving the go-ahead from the MoAg, the Ministry of Health (MoH) and the local council the dustmen set about their self-appointed task and began their club. It was an immediate success and within three weeks of its establishment the dustmen were finding that they had a huge surplus which enabled them to supply some 10 tons of feed to other pig dealers in addition to providing for their own animals. This success was trumpeted in the media, including the BBC, and was held up as an example to other corporations, many of which immediately set up their own schemes.

The pig clubs were a massive success and by the summer of 1943 there were believed to be more than 5,000 separate clubs in Britain with some 120,000 pigs being raised by the 110,000 members. By the end of the war the pig clubs were responsible for producing some 10,000 tons of meat every year.

The keeping of poultry also proved hugely popular. With the shortage of eggs being a chronic problem throughout the war, the keeping of hens grew massively. By 1945 the Domestic Poultry Keepers' Council had over 1,250,000 members and in 1943–1944 domestic poultry keepers were responsible for the production of over a quarter of all of the known supply of eggs. Of course, many eggs were not officially known about and there was a thriving black-market trade.

In order to prevent those private individuals who kept poultry from profiteering through the selling of surplus eggs while still making a profit, the Ministry of Food also issued an order in July which fixed maximum prices for the sale of home-produced eggs. The prices were divided according to category but had to conform to the individual weight standards which had been issued previously.

Home-Produced Eggs, Maximum Prices (per dozen)

Category	S	d
1A	2	9
1B	2	6
1C	2	3
1D	2	

Chapter 3

Rationing, Shortages and Controls

Feeling the way towards rationing

Rationing began, after governmental indecision had initially delayed it, in January 1940 with the imposition of butter and sugar restrictions. These were followed in quick succession by the rationing of meat and sugar and, by July 1941, the ration had extended to cover tea, margarine, and cooking fats. Preserves and cheeses were added to the rationed goods list in 1941. The rationing of cheese caused consternation in rural areas where many agricultural workers depended upon cheese for the majority of their meals and there were campaigns urging the government to allow extra cheese rations for such workers.

After the First World War the Committee of Imperial Defence was given the role of investigating food controls in the event of a future war. The committee recognised that valuable lessons had been learned during the First World War and that a policy of 'business as usual', as had been in place for the first years of the First World War, was completely unworkable in relation to a modern total war situation. Policies concerning food controls during the Second World War were heavily influenced by the British experiences of the First World War. The successes of the food control scheme of the First World War remained fresh in the memories of many of those who were now confronted by an outwardly appearing similar situation. Foremost amongst those influenced by previous policy was Sir William Beveridge who chaired the highly influential 1936 Sub-Committee on Food Supply in Time of War and was also the first permanent secretary to the Ministry of Food. The final report of Beveridge's sub-committee emphasised that any future policy of rationing would only succeed if 'each consumer was assured his or her share.'[1]

The proposed scheme of rationing and controls in the event of a future war was so complex that it was imperative that plans were made in advance. In order to facilitate this planning the Board of Trade Food (Defence Plans) Department was formed. This department organised the planning of both a scheme of supply control and methods of regulating consumer demand. As part of the plan the country was separated into regions and the local authorities were asked to establish local food control committees while Divisional Food Officers were appointed to administer the system during war.

The preparations for the rationing system were immense. The administrative burden alone was monumental and required huge numbers of volunteers. In Edinburgh, the writing up of food rationing cards for every resident of the Edinburgh area was just one of the monumental tasks which needed to be speedily but accurately completed. The convenor of the local Food Control Committee, Councillor G.D. Brown, relied upon a small army of civilian volunteers and by the end of October the task had been completed. Councillor Brown thanked the volunteers profusely and Mr George White, who had been largely responsible for the initial organisation of the volunteers, also praised the work undertaken while the Rev. D.W.P. Strang praised the work of the many volunteers from church organisations who had undertaken a large share of the work in various church halls. At the end of the meeting to thank the volunteers a collection was taken with the proceeds going to the Red Cross.

For the average Briton rationing meant that they were forced to register with specific retailers to obtain certain goods. This often resulted in large queues at local food control offices as housewives and others surged to put their names down with a favoured local survivor.

One of the more unusual results of the preparations for rationing was that meals had to be officially separated and categorised into breakfast, lunch, dinner and tea. Breakfast was classed as a substantial meal which included porridge or cereal, and fish, bacon, egg or sausage. For those who preferred a lighter repast and ate only bread or toast with butter or margarine and, perhaps, jam, in the morning the government classed their meal as being of the tea type rather than breakfast. This was important as it was decided that workers should have breakfast, lunch (often a packed lunch with the inevitable cheese sandwich or pie), dinner, and a teatime snack. All of this was to be accompanied by five hot drinks per day.

The main, substantial, meals had to include fish, game, eggs, meat or poultry alongside potatoes, vegetables and perhaps one or two other courses consisting of a starter (often soup or broth) and a pudding. This was rather ambitious in reality and diet varied according to availability of supplies, location and, in some cases, wealth. Meat pies, sandwiches (often, of course, cheese) and other forms of snack served without accompanying courses counted officially as subsidiary meals.[2]

Farmers were allowed the luxury of extra tea, sugar and milk for their workforce but this had to brewed and doled out communally. The hot beverages which were mentioned in official papers were described as being drinks which would traditionally be accompanied by sugar. Away from the fields, in industries in which the extra ration was also supplied a tea-maker would be appointed and would be responsible for not only brewing the tea but also with doling out the single spoonful of sugar to each eligible worker. This was often exploited and an extra spoon would be added to a tin which when full would be taken home to be used in jam-making.

One of the problems faced by those who were responsible for administering the rationing scheme was that of providing sufficient calorific content to those who were employed in hard manual labour or who worked in occupations which meant that they had limited access to full meals, cooking facilities, canteens or restaurants. It was recognised early on that agricultural workers were one group that fell into this bracket. The solution advanced by the authorities was an extra ration of cheese for these workers. The amount of this extra ration varied widely throughout the war. In early 1941 it was just 8oz while it reached its highest point in July 1942 when the extra ration stood at 16oz (double the domestic ration allocation) but this did not last long and just six months later it had fallen to 12oz.

Cheese was a dietary staple for such workers and had been for many decades before the war but in wartime Britain the supply of milk was such that the vast majority was used up for other purposes. As a result of this the majority of cheese had to be imported and imports of this commodity increased by 17 per cent to 93 per cent in 1944. Most of the imported cheese came from Canada, Australia, New Zealand and the USA.

It was not only the workers in fields and forestry who benefited from this extra ration. The categories of workers with such an entitlement was actually quite a long one and there were some surprising entries such as Ordnance Survey Field Revisers and full-time water bailiffs. Other entries were more those to be expected such as agricultural workers (and ancillary trades), canal workers and boatmen, coal borers, miners (employed underground) and coal distributors, electrical linesmen and those employed laying gas mains, for example. The full list extended to thirty-nine different categories of worker.

The MoF faced a huge challenge throughout the war. Rationing was by its nature restrictive and dependent upon availability of supplies but at the same time the MoF had to ensure that the British people were not deprived of ingredients which they had come to depend upon and felt strongly about. The British were a conservative people, by and large, and it proved immensely difficult to get them to change their dietary habits.

A list of ingredients which were seen as sacrosanct to the British public included bread, cheese, fats, flour, meats, milk, potatoes and other vegetables. Coming a close second to these items were eggs and fish while the traditional British addiction to tea was also held to be sacrosanct. Tea was seen as a special case as it was felt to be worthwhile for its comforting value in a crisis.

It was clear to local authorities that rationing, once put in place, would have a severe impact on ordinary life. Preparations for this were already in an advanced stage of planning throughout 1939 and local authorities solicited the aid of a variety of food producers, experts and associations to aid them in their onerous tasks with relation to rationing. In the early days of the war, for example, more than 150 Sunderland meat traders met at the Palatine Hotel to discuss the creation of a wartime butchers' association. The Deputy Meat Agent for town and district, Mr S.P. Goodfellow, presided over the meeting. Mr Goodfellow told his fellow traders that in this time of national crisis it behoved them to pull together and to act in a united way to benefit the whole community rather than work for the advantage of individuals. The National Federation of Meat Traders had urged the creation of Retail Butchers' Committees which would act as bulk buying groups for all butchers in their areas. The members voted unanimously in favour of forming such a group and elected Mr J. Dinsdale as president. It was agreed that two buying committees would be formed, one for the south side of the river and one for the north.[3]

Councillor R.G. Smart put it to the membership that it might be favourable to consider the earlier closing of their shops, at sunset, as a security measure and economy and this was favourably accepted. Concluding the meeting, the other Deputy Meat Agent, Mr Harry Dixon, explained that he and Mr Goodfellow were also responsible for other outlying areas, including Boldon, Herrington, Houghton-le-Spring, Ryhope and Silksworth, and had already held meetings in these outlying districts.

At the same time as the Retail Butchers' Committee was being formed the local authority were also considering matters concerning food supplies. The Town Council, under the auspices of the General Purposes Committee, set up a Food Control Committee which would oversee many of the aspects of rationing and the supply of food in the town. The committee comprised fifteen people made up of five representatives of the food trades and ten who were to represent the consumer. The five food trade representatives were: Mr T. M. Stores (representing the grocers and provisions dealers); Councillor R. G. Smart (butchers and fleshers); Mr Robert Whitfield (Co-operative Society); Mr G. Muirhead (fish trade); and Mr J. Earnshaw (bakery trade). The consumer representatives were: the mayor (Councillor Myers Wayman); Aldermen Cairns, Embleton and Summerbell; and Councillors Crow, Huggins, Semple, Patrick, Bell and Young. The General Purposes Committee also set up an advisory committee for the rationing of coal, gas and electricity and the Borough Treasurer, Mr F. Wilcox, was appointed as Fuel Overseer to act in conjunction with the members of the committee.

One commodity which was to be immediately rationed was petrol. The government had also decided that, with the harvest in full swing, the fuel rationing would not immediately apply to farmers – with the proviso that when they were buying fuel they must be able to satisfy the supplier that they would be using the petrol for the sole purpose of agriculture and would have to sign a receipt for all fuel purchased. This exception also applied to vans and lorries that were operating under agricultural licences but, farmers were strictly warned, did not apply to private, personal transport.

In the days leading up to the imposition of the petrol rationing system, reports came in that some people in the Aberdeen area were hoarding fuel by collecting it in drums and other large containers. Those who were considering this were sternly warned by the fuel officer that storing petrol without the necessary licence was an offence and that magistrates could impose a fine of £20 for each day the petrol had been stored.

Rationing and Shortages

Rationing came into force on 8 January when bacon, butter, ham, and sugar were rationed. The initial sugar ration was set at 12oz, while the others were all set at just 4oz. The imposition of rationing was heralded by a massive press campaign which sought to reassure people that rationing was for their own good and that it would ensure that everyone would receive a fair share regardless of their economic situation.

The first day of rationing passed relatively smoothly although there were many cases of customers forgetting to bring along their ration books and having to go back to get them. Many shopkeepers (grocers especially) at first found it easier to tear out an entire page of coupons to be crossed out as used rather than snipping out individual coupons for every customer (something which was later heavily discouraged) and criticised the fact that the pages were not perforated. Other problems encountered included many customers who had not filled in their names and address on the individual pages.

With the initial roll-out of rationing having gone as smoothly as could have been expected and with the general public largely supportive the initial foods were followed on 11 March by the introduction of a meat ration. In comparison to the earlier foods, however, the meat ration was apportioned by monetary value. Once again, most housewives (who in the Britain of 1940 did the majority of shopping) found that the scheme operated fairly smoothly. There were, of course, some problems. Most of these revolved around the fact that there was some confusion over whether or not the ration could be taken on separate days. The initial meat ration per adult was set at 1s 10d per week with a child's at 11d. The coupons were divided into four for the week thus meaning that each coupon was worth 5½d. Anxious shoppers were assured that their butchers could cut meat into such portions and they could therefore shop over several days or one as they desired. There was a catch, however. To cut meat into such small portions many joints would have to be boned and thus the boned cuts would be more expensive than bone-in.

Not all meat was initially placed on ration. Offal such as liver, kidney, tripe, heart and ox-tail were not rationed. Neither were sausages and pies which contained no more than 50 per cent meat. Poultry and game were also exempted but shoppers were warned that there was not an unlimited supply of these meats and were urged to shop early in the day. Shoppers were also urged not to blame their butcher if they could not always obtain what they wanted as it was to be expected that from time to time there might be shortages of particular meats or cuts.

As 1940 progressed and the war continued to go badly it was inevitable that other items would be placed on ration. In July there was some consternation when the nation's favourite, tea, was added at just 2oz per week. From 22 July margarine was also brought onto the ration and housewives were told that if they were already registered with a retailer for their butter ration then they need take no further action but that if they were not already registered then they should register with a suitable retailer immediately. Some Orcadians preferred to register for their butter supply direct from local farmers and they were assured that they would be able to collect their 6oz weekly butter ration in farm butter from 22 July.

There was some relief, however, as everyone with a ration card was informed that they could draw an extra ration of 2lbs of sugar during July as long as the sugar was only used for the purpose of preserving fruit. Thus, for example, a family of four would be entitled to receive an extra 8lbs of sugar for jam-making or the bottling of fruit. Although the majority of housewives were considering jam-making they were urged to instead consider bottling fruit as it was the best way of preserving large stocks of precious fruit for long-term use. In order to aid the housewife who was considering bottling fruit for the first time the Ministry of Agriculture published a pamphlet, costing 4d, entitled *Preserves from the Garden*. The pamphlet included complete and concise instructions on the making of jams and jellies, the bottling, canning and pulping of fruit, the drying of fruit and vegetables, and recipes for the preparation of chutneys, pickles, fruit cheeses and so on. The pamphlet also gave full instructions for the preparation of jars suitable for the purpose of preserving.

The importance of rationing in the British wartime experience cannot be overestimated. On Tyneside, as throughout Britain, in 'contrast with air raids or evacuation, rationing and shortages affected everybody'.[4] The austerity measures that were a direct result of rationing were accepted by the vast majority of the British public and were viewed as a necessity of war. This view was reinforced by the favour that was shown to the theory of fair shares for all and dissatisfaction was most often the result of perceived inequalities within the system. The extensive propaganda campaign, exhorting the public to be stoically self-sacrificing appears to have been largely successful with the majority remaining supportive of rationing as a necessary wartime measure.

Lord Woolton was in many ways the perfect man for the job of Minister of Food. Widely recognised and praised for his bluff but down-to-earth and friendly manner he also had the skillset which was required in this complex role. As a former social worker and owner of a chain of stores he understood the food retail business and knew of the deprived state of many of Britain's poorest. One of the very first questions he asked when he took up his post was to enquire who the scientific officer was. Woolton was eager to get more thrusting scientists into the ministry and he chose Professor J.C. Drummond as his scientific adviser. Drummond had been seconded to the MoF in October 1939 from his role as Professor of Biochemistry at University College London. He and his wife had co-authored a classic history of English diet and Woolton saw him as the perfect candidate as he possessed a knowledge of both nutrition and the British diet. He was also, like Woolton, a crusading reformer. Drummond was perhaps the key man in persuading both Woolton and Churchill that if the rationing scheme was to work it required not only the support of the public but also of the retail and food industries. Other key proposals made by Drummond included using the war as an opportunity to improve the nutrition of pregnant women and children from poorer families and in ensuring that there was no repeat of the disastrous First World War campaign to encourage the people to eat less bread.

The imposition of rationing had some initial teething troubles. One of these was criticism over the butter ration. March 1940 brought welcome news that the butter ration was to be doubled. For the grocery trade this was welcome news as they had been calling for an adjustment to the ration. In Edinburgh, traders argued that this new arrangement would not affect supplies in the city as they felt that many in the working-class areas of the city would not take up the full ration as they had already made the adjustment to margarine and found this quite suitable for most tasks.

In Edinburgh the Ministry of Food was warning of an impending shortage of eggs in Edinburgh which was expected to hit in autumn and winter. Although eggs were currently available the prices had increased but as supplies from Denmark had been cut off it was thought that it might become necessary to ration eggs when the local supplies began to dry up. There were concerns being expressed by Edinburgh housewives that the price of eggs might soar in the event of a shortage while it had become common for many residents to leave the city at weekend for country areas in order to secure supplies of eggs. However, a leading Edinburgh egg retailer was keen to reassure the public that there was little likelihood of an impending price rise and told customers that supplies were being bolstered by eggs from northern Scotland and from Ireland. The loss of the Danish market had also led to a shortfall in the supply of bacon and butter.

A review which reported in May 1940 saw Drummond recommend that better use must be made of grain. As part of this he suggested using 85 per cent of grain in flour for baking bread. Drummond's review also suggested increasing the production of milk and vegetables, including, crucially, potatoes. A key part of Drummond's argument was to reduce shipping space which was given over to what he saw as nutritionally wasteful foods. He therefore suggested drastically reducing the amount of fresh fruit, meat and eggs which were shipped to Britain. These would be replaced by greater imports of canned fish, cheese, condensed and powdered milk and dried pulses. The suggestions were, by and large, enacted upon and in the middle years of the war, 1942–1944, the importation of fresh fruit had declined by 90 per cent. A further suggestion was that urgent efforts should be made to secure supplies of concentrates of vitamins A and D which could be added to margarine. Some MoF advice was well thought out while some was more well-intentioned than acted upon, such as the suggestion in some newspapers that cooled water which had been used to boil turnip could be given to babies to provide additional Vitamin C.

Woolton and Drummond agreed on many key aspects of policy. One of these was the necessity to carry out a very extensive public relations campaign which encouraged the housewife that careful cooking methods could help the war effort, and also to encourage people to support the rationing scheme and to Dig for Victory. Drummond espoused this view as he knew that greater nutrition could only be obtained through changes while it appealed to Woolton due to his previous experience as a freelance journalist.

Although often seen as being detrimental to morale, rationing could provide a boost to the wellbeing of some. These were usually those better off, with a social conscience or a developed sense of patriotism. For such individuals rationing was one way in which they could achieve a sense of sacrifice, participation, and shared communal experience.[5] The policy of developing factory canteens stemmed solely from the policy of ensuring that workers had access to nutritious meals, it also created a boost in production by ensuring that workers took shorter breaks and remained on site during these meal breaks. This was a morale boosting development for workers in that it allowed them to maintain their morale while engaged in important war work.

In a clear demonstration of widespread support for the rationing system, the demand from the public throughout the early years of the war was that they wanted more goods placed on the ration list in order to ensure fair shares. At the very beginning of rationing there had been a great deal of anger directed towards restaurants. At first these establishments were exempt from rationing and people quickly perceived that this meant that the wealthy who could afford to regularly dine out could evade the fairness of rationing.

The government responded by limiting restaurants to serving meals costing no more that 5s. Even so, discontent towards restaurant owners and customers continued throughout the war. This was largely because of a perception amongst the public that restaurants and hotels were 'cornering supplies of un-rationed commodities'.[6]

For such a huge change to the British way of life the government managed to bring in a system which was remarkably simple to understand and operate. The key to this was a lack of differentiation, the vast majority of older children and adults received the same ration. As we shall see, this did sometimes cause resentment but the government relented in the case of agricultural workers and miners who were allocated extra cheese. Retailers of rationed goods received supplies which were linked with the number of customers that they had on their register. To buy rationed goods a customer presented his or her ration book to the retailer who cancelled the relevant coupons and returned the book to the customer.

On Tyneside the shortages were beginning to be felt as early as April 1940 when Newcastle City Police noted increasing public concerns over the shortages of both eggs, which were not rationed, and beef, which had been rationed only the previous month.[7] As the war intensified the public appear to have been more willing to accept scarcities and rationing. So that, by the crisis point of September 1940, it was widely believed that the majority of the public accepted the shortages of eggs and the meagreness of the butter ration as 'a fact of the wartime economy'.[8]

It is clear, however, that the public grew increasingly irritable if shortages of a particular commodity continued for several consecutive weeks. This was clearly demonstrated across Tyneside when, after the aforementioned shortages of eggs continued into October 1940, complaints about both this and, once again, the meagre butter ration surfaced with renewed vigour.[9] Grievances regarding shortages of meat, eggs, and onions, continued on into the first few months of 1941.[10] Across Britain the shortage of onions proved to be one of the most contentious aspects of the home front.[11] Although this was the worst period of the war it would seem that the shortages were still not fully accepted by the public despite the earlier optimism of the police intelligence reports. Indeed, the situation on Tyneside was worsening with an increasing level of dissatisfaction being voiced over the uneven distribution of food.

It would appear that the shortages had reached such a level that the Tyneside public were beginning to lose faith in the entire system of fair shares for all rationing. More worryingly for the authorities, this was further demonstrated by the founding of the Newcastle Housewives Guild (NHG) in March 1941. The NHG was heavily backed and influenced by the support of the local branch of the British Communist Party (BCP) making the authorities highly suspicious of its activities. The NHG began to campaign for greater supplies of foodstuffs. Complaints were, however, in proportion and seldom approached levels of concern. In common with national surveys the main focus of complaints on Tyneside was based on the inequalities and profiteering that the system permitted. Complaints also arose over the quality of meat that was being made available for human consumption and by May 1940 these complaints had reached such a level that the matter was being discussed by the Newcastle, Gateshead and District Butchers' Association.[12]

Throughout 1941 the situation caused by food rationing was beginning to reach critical levels and the government and local authorities were looking for alternatives which would allow people (especially those engaged on important work) to have access to nourishing meals. Perhaps the most successful of these enterprises was the establishment of numerous British Restaurants which gave nutritious and cheap meals at low cost to customers. In Alnwick, Northumberland, a British Restaurant was opened by the Duchess of Northumberland and was an immediate success in the town. Councillor Stone declared that as a regular customer he could vouch for the service and said that many workmen used the restaurant between 12 and 1 p.m. and that others who had more flexible lunch hours should stagger their visits. Councillor Stone declared that the manageress was very efficient and that the waitresses 'were nippy and cheerful'.[13]

Rationing had a large impact on the children. With the rationing of sugar came an, at first, unofficial rationing of sweets and cakes, while lack of fresh fruit meant that many children growing up during the war, especially those in urban areas, had little recollection of what an orange or a banana looked like. This was a national norm: one doctor in Westmoreland was called out to a suspected appendicitis only to discover that the child had eaten her first orange and, never having seen one before, had eaten it peel and all.[14] Obtaining extra sweet coupons from a relative or friend became the highlight of many children's war. Children with spare pocket money clubbed together to share sweets while the first day of the new butter ration was anticipated for the thicker than usual layers of butter on the bread, the greyish-brown national loaf which was much disliked, at breakfast. Some children supplemented their ration through theft and local farmers were plagued by the pilfering of turnips and apples. One man, a young boy in North Shields at the time, recalls frequent hunger motivated trips to the farm at nearby Preston village to steal turnips.

Worries over the deterioration of children's diet due to rationing were one of the foremost concerns shared by both the general public and by the government. By 1941 eggs and milk, while not officially rationed, had become controlled goods. Eighteen per cent of the country's milk supply was set aside for priority goods.[15] This was a measure largely designed to ensure an adequately balanced diet for the most vulnerable groups in society. This vulnerable group included expectant mothers, recent mothers, adolescents and invalids, but it was primarily aimed at young children. The result of increased supplies for children did result in the government being unable to guarantee items for ordinary people, due to seasonal and regional fluctuation.

On the whole wartime rationing was, despite the anxieties of parents and government, largely beneficial for children, especially those who came from working-class homes. The British Medical Association (BMA) reported that, when compared to the pre-war data, children in 1944 were both taller and heavier; a sign of better overall health standards. However, this was balanced by the fact that rates of death from tuberculosis had increased when compared to pre-war figures and this remained a major concern for the BMA. Despite this one, albeit large, concern, anthropometric survey clearly indicated that there were significant improvements in the general health of children during the war and that, as well as the increase in mean heights and weights, there was a 'substantial improvement in child health ... as well as the virtual elimination of many of the extreme forms of physical disability'.[16]

In 1941, the rationed list extended to include items such as jam, marmalade, syrup, and treacle (8oz each), cheese (initially 1oz but a month later increased to 2oz), and controls were placed on milk consumption. By the end of 1941 the points rationing system was further extended with several canned foods, including meat, fish and vegetables, being added to the list of rationed goods. Rather than being seen as a restriction, however, the move was broadly welcomed as being long overdue with many people having long complained that the more well off had been cornering the market in items such as tinned salmon.

The following year saw even more items added to the rationed list. In January dried fruit, pulses, rice, sago and tapioca were added. These were followed in April by breakfast cereal and condensed milk, in July by syrup, in August by biscuits and in December by oatflakes and rolled oats. One of the most unpopular items to be added in 1942 (especially amongst the younger generation) was chocolate and sweets which became rationed in July.

One side-effect of the rationing system and subsequent shortages of some non-rationed goods was an increase in queuing. Such was the extent of queues that they rapidly became something of a problem to those in authority who were anxious that they led to the spread of rumours and encouraged idleness. In early August 1941 the local press in

Northumberland carried an article which claimed that the problem was a distinctly British one which had been exacerbated by the shortages of non-rationed goods such as canned goods, chocolate and biscuits along with seasonal items such as tomatoes. The article hinted that a possible solution being considered by the Minister of Food was to extend the rationed goods list to include some of these items. The article also urged people to gain a sense of perspective when it came to rationed goods and claimed that rationed items 'will wait until you call for them' but ignored the effects that black-market activities and shortages sometimes had with numerous examples of stores running out of even rationed items when they clearly should not have.

By the summer of 1942 the average British subject was entitled to just 1s 2d of meat (beef, mutton, pork or veal) every week but other sources of meat, such as rabbit, poultry and venison, remained off ration and a useful alternative for those who were lucky enough to be able to obtain them. This resulted in each person being able to obtain approximately 1lb of rationed meat per week but the amount fluctuated with prices.

In the same period rations stood at 4oz bacon and ham/week; 8oz sugar; 8oz fats (half of which had to be margarine while 2oz could be butter and 2oz cooking fats); 8oz cheese; 16oz of jam, marmalade or sweet mincemeat every four weeks; 8oz of sweets every four weeks; and one packet of dried eggs (equivalent to a dozen eggs) every eight weeks. Most of these were fairly stable but the cheese ration fluctuated widely during 1943 and 1944, when it fell to just 2oz per week in April. Fresh eggs were not widely available and most people could expect no more than one every fortnight if they were lucky. For this rare and much sought after commodity a system of distribution similar to that used for milk was put into place. This gave priority to expectant and nursing mothers, children and to certain invalids. Each adult also was given 20 points to spend on a fairly wide variety of goods. Prices for these items varied widely.

Several key ingredients such as bread, fish, fruit, potatoes and vegetables were not rationed and this was shown to be wise when a survey in 1944 estimated that the average housewife was spending 9s in every £1 (or almost half) on unrationed goods. A further 2s was being spent on points-rationed items but the vast majority of the remaining 9s was spent on rationed goods.

Complaints over the rationing system and food shortages in the later war period seem to have been largely confined to localised problems. The most serious complaint of the later war period on Tyneside would appear to have arisen around March 1942 when there were complaints that green vegetables were only available to those who could 'afford them'.[17] It is perhaps significant that a memo from the Ministry of Food was sent to Newcastle Corporation at this time saying that a door-to-door survey into food supplies would be carried out in May.[18] Further problems arose when allotment holders attempted to purchase extra vegetables and were forced to complain that local greengrocers were refusing to serve them as they had not been registered as customers with them during previous years. However, by September 1944 the region's food stocks were sufficient to provide adequate food for its own population but also for large numbers of evacuees from the south of the country.[19]

Although the vast majority of Britons were generally supportive of the rationing system there were local inconsistencies which could spark resentment. The BCP was one organisation which was prepared to speak out about what it saw as the various elements of unfairness within the rationing system. The party continued its policy of representing the working man and his family by organising voluntary pressure groups, such as the NHG, to campaign for greater food supplies or better air raid shelters and by opening advice centres in the aftermath of heavy air raids.[20] The NHG was a small organisation which campaigned on all of these issues but which focused on the need for greater rations being made available to areas which were traditionally employed in heavy and labour-intensive industries. Most of the organisations and campaigns organised by the BCP, however, were viewed by many, and especially by the authorities, as being trouble-makers.

The rationing of food impacted not only on the food retail sector and the customer, but also the butchery trade. Even before the system was actually imposed butchers were faced with having to get used to having established lists of customers, to sell meat using different methods according to government-assigned prices and to cope with a sometimes bewildering series of new regulations governing their trade. Shortages of meat and the implementation of coupons meant that those in this trade faced several new challenges brought about by the war. The centralisation of slaughterhouses was one such new phenomenon. In many places there were initial difficulties to be overcome. For example, just three such establishments were meant to cater for the majority of the north-east of England and this resulted in supplies of meat on Tyneside running short on several occasions. Reacting to this new imposition, the members of the Newcastle, Gateshead and District Butchers' Association vehemently criticised the measure and claimed that the scheme would be unworkable. A deputation was sent to protest to the Ministry of Food and the policy was decried as a recipe for disaster that would 'make no end of confusion'.[21]

Early in the war, however, the main complaint seems to not have been regarding quantity but quality of meat provided by butchers as there were several complaints that meat supplied was of a poor grade.[22] One of the most common complaints concerned the profiteering of butchers around the Christmas period when the prices of turkeys and other fowl tended to increase. On Tyneside there were several complaints about this matter from members of the general public and the association promised to hold a full internal inquiry with punishment for any member who was found to be profiteering.[23] During the Christmas of 1940 the level of complaints regarding this matter reached such a level that they were included in the police intelligence reports, it was said that people believed the prices to be 'exorbitant'.[24]

The announcement that sweets and chocolate would be rationed from 26 July 1942 brought undoubted consternation to British children but the announcement four days before rationing was due to begin that the ration would be just 2oz per week also led to dismay amongst confectioners. There was much discussion amongst the confectionary trade in Edinburgh as to whether or not the ration was too meagre. Some claimed that this was indeed the case and it would lead to a drastic drop in sales and income. Some confectioners claimed that the scheme was uneconomic as it would result in a wastage of paper bags and would increase the workloads of staff and argued that instead of a weight ration it would have been better to set the ration at 6d per person. Sweet manufacturers, on the other hand, claimed that the ration was to be expected and had come as no surprise to them given the rationing on sugar. The government proceeded carefully ensuring that at the end of the first month of sweet rationing there would be a surplus supply of sweets so that the ration could be adjusted according to demand and public reaction to the ration. The trade reported that they could reasonably expect 10–20 per cent of the population to forgo their sweet ration altogether but this could not be guaranteed. There had clearly been a problem prior to the ration as one confectioner, while otherwise arguing against the harshness of the ration, said that it would at least 'stop the activities of "shop crawlers", who spent their time collecting all the sweets they could get while others had to go without'.[25]

As well as this there was no guarantee that the meat was fit for consumption due to the unethical practices of some shopkeepers. One young woman queued for over four hours just to purchase a rabbit and some biscuits. Despite her determination, when she returned home, she discovered that the rabbit was rotten and inedible.[26] Some retailers demonstrated favouritism towards certain customers and sale of under the counter goods was commonplace. A young boy at the time recalled a greengrocer declaring to his mother that he had no fruit and then later giving a large bag of fruit to a woman who had no children. Such unfairness and cheating of the system would appear to have been relatively commonplace, despite the fact that it was illegal.

In 1943 the MoAg continued in its efforts to encourage housewives (and others) to try to make the best of what was available in order to prepare nutritious meals for themselves and their families amongst severe shortages. The national and local press continually carried various recipes which made use of easily available ingredients, often vegetables which could be grown at home. At the end of April 1943, for example, the *Berwick Advertiser* carried three recipes which had recently been demonstrated at a show in London. The recipes were for leek pudding served with either gravy or a cheese sauce, vegetable hot-pot made using leeks or onions, carrots, turnips and potatoes, and a dish which was called 'spring victory' and which consisted of carrots, turnip, swede, spring onions and powdered egg served with a white sauce.

Manufacturers of tinned foods also got in on the act by placing adverts in the press which made attempts to give readers new methods of using their products. Fray Bentos, for example, ran a series of adverts throughout the spring of 1943 in which recipes for corned beef pie and corned beef turnover were given (see Appendix 1).

Christmas brought with it extra pressure to ensure that not only was there sufficient food but that there also remained some semblance of celebration. To this end many housewives were inspired by ideas from the press in order to creatively make use of what was available. We have already seen how, in some locations, off-ration meats such as venison replaced hard to obtain turkey. Fuel for cooking was also sometimes a problem and as Christmas 1943 approached the *Berwick Advertiser* ran an article advising housewives (the article was entitled 'Of Interest to Women') how to prepare a Christmas or New Year feast for those who possessed only basic cooking equipment or a coal fire. The menu that was suggested included a course of stuffed meat such as veal served with boiled vegetables, potatoes, steamed sprouts and gravy. This was to be followed by Christmas pudding and custard.

We have already seen how the authorities attempted to ensure that rationing was handled in as simple a way as possible but by the latter years of the war, with more and more goods rationed, this was not always possible. The periodic issuance of new ration books was always a rather fraught time and depended largely upon the competence of the authorities and the compliance of the local community. The issue of new ration books in Aberdeen resulted in some confusion on 23 May

1944 with large queues forming at Aberdeen Music Hall. People had been told, by area and street, on which day they should attend to collect their new ration books. The authorities also encouraged a 'good neighbour' policy whereby people could collect ration books for neighbouring families, but also explained that people should be sensible about this and not collect too many books as this might cause delays. On the day when the problems ensued the Food Executive Officer, Mr A. Drysdale, explained that the problems had largely been caused by people attending on the incorrect day, while further delays had been caused by people who had not signed their identity cards or had failed to complete the reference page of their old ration book(s). Such problems were of great concern as they not only affected the nation's food supply preparations but also could erode morale in local areas if people lost faith in the rationing system.

Alternatives to the Ration

In addition to the many who were digging for victory, and joining pig or poultry clubs, there were other sources of food for the enterprising. It was quickly put forward that more should be made of the wild harvest which was often freely available, albeit more commonly in rural areas. Although the foraging skills remained honed in many areas there were also many people who had lost the skills necessary to benefit from foraging the woods and hedgerows. In recognition of this, and of the dangers inherent in the practice if attempted by the unskilled, County Herb Committees were set up by the MoAg to give advice about what wild foods could be eaten safely. The MoF also got in on the act by issuing pamphlets and guidance on how to get the best out of gathered food. Anyone who wanted to benefit from official advice could send for a MoF leaflet entitled *Hedgerow Harvest*. This handy publication contained much useful advice including recipes for jams and preserves, as well as advice on storing various items including mushrooms.

Loading the hay crop at Plymouth Central Park. (*Western Morning News*)

Householders applying to change their designated retailers at Newcastle Food Control Office, 1941. (*Evening Chronicle*)

National Fire Service, London, fruit and veg display. (*Illustrated Sporting and Dramatic News*)

National Fire
Service's pig pens
(*Illustrated Sporting
and Dramatic News*)

Above left: Judging the rabbit section. (*Illustrated Sporting
and Dramatic News*)

Above right: Miss Betty Reid of the Women's Land Army.
(*The Scotsman*)

Left: Land girl ploughing at Liss.
(*Portsmouth Evening News*)

Wartime cookery demo advertisement. (*Lancaster*)

Stork margarine ad for 'veal and ham' pie. (*Belfast Telegraph*)

Gloucester pig club members with their charges. (*Gloucester Journal*)

Above: Mr Cedric Drewe, MP, and members of the London Zookeepers' Pig Club. (*Western Morning News*)

Below: Pig club members off to work. (*Illustrated Sporting and Dramatic News*)

IT'S OFF TO WORK WE GO : *A group of club members set out from the communal tool-shed. For convenience sake, every member has his own key.*

Above left: Pig pens are shown off to senior officers. (*Illustrated Sporting and Dramatic News*)

Above right: Young pig looked over by PC Dipper (r). (*Illustrated Sporting and Dramatic News*)

Below left: Inspector Bartlett and the Minister of Agriculture enjoy a cup of tea. (*Illustrated Sporting and Dramatic News*)

Below right: PC Beck inspects his peas. (*Illustrated Sporting and Dramatic News*)

Sgt C. Bunnell thins his onions. (*Illustrated Sporting and Dramatic News*)

PC Tipping at work on his allotment. (*Illustrated Sporting and Dramatic News*)

PC Stantion cutting down thistles to prepare another allotment plot. (*Illustrated Sporting and Dramatic News*)

Above left: Sir Phillip Game (r) and Superintendent Purbrick. (*Illustrated Sporting and Dramatic News*)

Above right: The Harrods piggery being inspected by Mr Drew and the Secretary of the Small Pig Keepers Council, Mr Alec Hobson. (*Illustrated Sporting and Dramatic News*)

Below: Lawns at Dundarach being ploughed up. (*Edinburgh Evening News*)

Above: Schoolboys from Loretto School helping with the harvest. (*The Scotsman*)

Left: Mr Lloyd Geroge is toasted by his farmworkers at a British Restaurant. (*The Sphere*)

Women of the semi mobile cooking unit. (*The Sphere*)

In 1940 a book entitled *They Can't Ration These* was published in Britain. The writer was a Free-Frenchman named Vicomte Georges de Mauduit. The Frenchman had previously published three cookery books and for his latest offering he had managed to persuade David Lloyd George to write the foreword. The book gave useful advice (although some of the ingredients would have been unavailable to many) and included recipes for nettle cake, and others using ingredients such as clover, sorrel, hops, pickled broom buds and wild fennel. Less useful advice included the introduction of grass as a vegetable in the human diet.[27]

Blackberries were the most popular wild harvest and children were often sent out on foraging expeditions to gather these berries or nuts in the autumn. With the increasing importance given to nutrition and vitamin content advertisements for recipes for rose-hip jam filled many publications but the making of this Vitamin C rich jam was not generally a success during the war years as it was very difficult to successfully strain out the irritant hairs which are found in the hips. Far more successful was the production of rose-hip syrup which could effectively be strained by even the uninitiated by the use of a jelly bag.

Wartime necessities, however, saw a vast increase in the variety of items foraged from the hedgerows. Elderberries, rowanberries and other edible fruits proved popular with housewives who were advised to consider making apple and elderberry jam, rowanberry conserve or to gather and dry bilberries and elderberries as a substitute for currants in baking. Juice pressed from crab apples provided a substitute for lemon juice. Early in the war the advice for those who had gathered nuts was to bury them in a tin with a tightfitting lid in order to store them for later but by 1942 the advice on preserving this harvest had changed and housewives were advised to store cobnuts or filberts in jars with an inch of salt while the more common walnuts and chestnuts could be stored in tins with a layer of sand.

Wild food was a very valuable resource but the government was at pains throughout the war to point out that such supplies should only be obtained legally. We have already seen how some members of the community took to poaching in order to obtain food supplies; this continued throughout the war. On 1 July 1941 a Bishop Auckland man, Arthur V. Knight, who was employed by the Forestry Commission on the banks of the River Alwin in Northumberland was observed by a local shepherd, Mr William Cook, paddling in the river and splashing in an effort to force fish into an area where he had placed three nets. When Mr Cook asked him what he was doing Knight answered that he was getting trout. Mr Cook then informed him that it was illegal and when Knight became abusive he forcibly took possession of the nets and reported Knight to the bailiffs. Knight wrote to the hearing saying that he was innocent, that the nets were not in his possession but merely lying at the bottom of the river and that he was being prosecuted out of vindictiveness. However, the poaching of salmon and trout had now reached the stage that the authorities were becoming increasingly concerned and were willing to make far harsher examples than they had earlier in the war. The solicitor acting for the prosecution thanked Mr Cook and said that such public spiritedness was vital at this time when 'bailiffs are being called up for active service' and asked the bench to make an example of such cases. The bench concurred in the seriousness of the offence and fined Mr Knight the sum of £2.

In December of the same year a haulage contractor, Mr George Norman Birkley, from Felton in Northumberland was charged with possession of poaching equipment (a gaff) with the intent to illegally kill salmon, trout or other fish on 1 November. A water bailiff had seen blood at the river bank and when one followed the trail he spotted two men attempting to hide; one of the men was carrying a 12- foot stick with a gaff on the end. The two men made a run for it but the bailiff pursued and apprehended the defendant before cautioning him that possession of a gaff was illegal as was the taking of fish out of season.

Mr Birkley pleaded not guilty and said that he had business with the miller (whose garden lay next to the mill-race) and that as the miller was not in he had decided to take a walk along the river to kill the time. After encountering the bailiff he claimed that he told him the reason for his presence and that, because the other man had gotten away, he was being made a scapegoat. Evidence from Mr Reeney of Woodburn House, West Thirston, would seem to have called into question the timescale of supposed events as he claimed that he saw the bailiff go up past with the stick earlier than he had said to have apprehended the accused. Despite this the court found Mr Birkley guilty of possession of the gaff but that he had not been seen using it and fined Mr Birkley the sum of £4 8s 6d.

Poaching for game remained a constant problem throughout the war and the authorities in Northumberland remained strict in their enforcement. In January 1943 a case at Alnwick heard how two men of Netherton Colliery and Bedlington respectively had been apprehended with ferrets, nets and several dead rabbits at Lesbury. Once again, the magistrates took a dim view of the affair and the two, Joseph Cavanagh and Walter Ellis, were fined £1 and £2 respectively.

Despite the efforts to grow more food in Britain, a great deal of food continued to be imported into the country, much of it from the USA. The Lend-Lease programme is more commonly associated with armaments and equipment but a great deal of food was also imported thanks to the scheme. Throughout the summer of 1941 shipments of bacon, beans, canned meat, cheese, dried eggs, evaporated milk, and lard began to arrive from across the Atlantic. The first such shipment arrived on 31 May and in 1941 Lend-Lease shipments constituted one-fifteenth of all food which arrived in Britain from abroad.

This was crucially important as early 1941 proved to be the worst period of the war in terms of diet. Food imports into Britain during this period were only 66 per cent of pre-war levels. The ploughing-up campaign was, as we have seen, a huge success but could only be achieved through a reduction in the numbers of livestock and by January 1941 the situation was so severe that the meat ration was reduced from the 2s 2d per week which it had reached in the summer of the previous year to just 1s 2d; a rate it remained at.

The Black Market

Given the stringencies of the rationing system it is no surprise that there were criminals who sought to exploit the system either to profit from the resale of rationed items or simply to obtain extras for themselves and their families. In December 1941 magistrates at Edinburgh heard a case involving the fraudulent use of ration books. The allegation was that between 1 April and 29 May 1940 a Mrs Violet Smith (also known as Potter or Johnston) of 9 Hay Avenue had stated to the authorities that two ration books from her household had been lost and she had been given replacements. She had then gone to her grocer on two or three occasions per week (using different ration books) to obtain rationed items for household members. The assistant who had served her did not know the details of Mrs Smith's household but the grocer himself had become suspicious and had reported the matter. Upon investigation the two books supposedly lost were discovered and that the names on them had been altered to Mrs Smith's married and maiden names. The court heard testimony from a handwriting expert who stated that the writing was Mrs Smith's and she was found guilty and sentenced to one month's imprisonment.

As we have seen, milk was another valuable commodity and in the same month as the above case was heard a Robina Ella Scott (also known as Chapman) of 9 Orwell Place, Edinburgh, admitted having obtained by fraudulent applications some 683 pints of free milk between 1 April and 25 October. Her defence argued that Scott's household income was only £3 3s per week (compared to an average of £5 3s 8½d) and that she had four children (aged between 1 and 5). Taking these things into consideration the sheriff was therefore asked to show leniency in his sentencing and merely impose a fine. The sheriff, however, stated that cases like this were becoming all too common and he could not show leniency before sentencing Scott to three weeks' imprisonment.

Many of those charged with black market offences were individual citizens concerning large numbers of firms, both large and small, also fell afoul of the law. In the summer of 1941 a Sunderland firm fell victim to the strict food regulations. Gallons Ltd were fined the sum of 10s for selling rationed food (cooking fats) to persons who were not registered with the firm. The incident involved the firm's branch on Dundas Street and revolved around a household of four persons who were registered at the shop for bacon, sugar and butter but not for cooking fats. It had been determined in May that Gallons had been supplying this household with cooking fats and when approached the manageress had explained that this had been an oversight on the part of the staff. It was accepted that there was no ulterior motive behind the offence and that it had been an honest mistake resulting, partially, from the lack of re-registration in January, but the firm was still fined.

Some of this criminal activity was highly organised and massively profitable but the vast majority of crimes brought before the courts involved single individuals or small groups. Juvenile criminals seem to have been particularly fond of purloining foodstuffs. In a typical example which was clearly encouraged by the potential profits to be made from the resale of food, there had been a rash of thefts from allotments, gardens and orchards in the Sunderland area. Testifying at Sunderland Juvenile Court in the prosecution of a 13-year-old boy accused of causing £3 of damage to an allotment owned by Mr George Evans of Chester Road, Chief Detective Inspector Middlemist stated that 'This type of offence is becoming very frequent, and I would ask the public to be very suspicious of young boys who come round the streets hawking lettuce and other similar things.' Mr Evans, who was an ex-serviceman, testified that he had suffered the theft, or loss through damage, of 350 heads of lettuce in the last few days. On one occasion Mr Evans had managed to apprehend the 13-year-old lad with 70 lettuces in a wheelbarrow. The boy had told him that he had acquired the lettuces from the school garden but at the police station he gave a false name and address. When he was later apprehended, the boy confessed to stealing the lettuces from the property of Mr Evans and had sold lettuces from a previous theft for a total of 3s. The chairman, Mr Williamson once more, placed the boy on probation for two years, ordered his father to pay Mr Evans the sum of £3 at a rate of 10s per week and bound him over in the sum of £5. Mr Williamson commented that he would have ordered the lad to be birched but that this would then have prevented him from ordering the repayment for the damage caused.

In common with most other areas of the country there was an extensive black market for foodstuffs on Tyneside with much of this being controlled by career criminals who used theft to obtain food stocks. One Newcastle family, however, found themselves black marketers through circumstance. The father was employed as a cook at a nearby military post where a clerical error had resulted in ten times the amount of food being supplied as was required. This food should have been either returned or destroyed but instead the cook collected the surplus and sold this on the black market around Newcastle. The family sold meat, eggs, butter, cheese, and other scarce foodstuffs to local businesses and private individuals, making a comfortable living in the process.[28] The culprits were never caught and the scheme only came to an end when their father was posted away.

We have previously seen the concerns over the activities of young people who were often left to their own devices during the war. In September 1941 there were several cases of youngsters from a number of south-east Northumberland communities damaging crops. These included the case of two Bedlington boys, aged 13 and 14, who were found guilty of damaging twenty pikes of hay at Hirst Head Farm. Fining the boys 10s apiece with damages of 5s apiece the magistrate admonished them, saying, 'There is a shortage of agricultural workers … They are working night and day to get food commodities put into the stores for the winter and you fellows come and pull them down … You should have been doing more useful work … This damage going on is a very serious business.'

Spurred on by shortages of food and by mischief there were also several cases of turnips being damaged or stolen and the instances of this crime were evidently increasing in frequency. Three Bedlington girls, aged 14 and 13, were found guilty of damaging turnips at Lane End Farm and fined 6s each. The girls were particularly unfortunate as the farm belonged to the District Officer for the War Agricultural Committee, Mr Charles R. Elliott, and he urged for a heavy punishment as a deterrent saying that, given his position, he was keenly aware of the necessity of producing as much food as possible and that warning signs had been placed at farms under the Defence of the Realm regulations. The bench concurred but added that they were 'sorry to see fine girls like you' before them.[29] At the same hearing two Cambois boys aged 12 and 15 were fined 11s each for a similar incident at Town Farm, East Sleekburn, and three Netherton Colliery girls aged 9, 12 and 13 were fined 5s 8d apiece for damaging turnips at South Farm, Nedderton.

Similar cases were also heard involving damage to crops of peas and oats at Brock Lane Farm, East Sleekburn. The farmer, Thomas Patterson, had caught the boys with the peas on them and found that a fair amount of damage had been done to the field. Admonishing the boys, he had told them to keep out of his fields in future. The chairman advised the boys to plant some peas in their own gardens to which one cheekily replied that there were already some peas in his garden and the chairman, who appears to have been slightly amused by this cheek, replied saying that the peas from the field 'must have been a bit sweeter than yours'.

Many of the black market and rationing offence cases brought before the various courts were fairly trivial in nature and were an example of ordinarily law-abiding folk falling victim of the huge numbers of new laws and regulations governing foodstuffs. Others, however, highlighted a darker side to British wartime society and demonstrated that vast profits could be made by those who were able to exploit the new system of regulations and laws.

A National Scandal, the Larmour Case

One of the keys to the successful implementation of the rationing scheme was that it provided fair shares for all. Despite this there were many who were ready to circumvent the scheme in order to obtain food either for themselves or to sell on at a profit. Despite the efforts of the police and the justice system there remained a thriving black-market in illicit food throughout the war and throughout the country.

In some cases black-market activities were highly organised and worked on a large scale for huge profits. Most black-market activities, however, were small in scale and ranged from shop owners favouring customers when it came to the ration to those who pilfered from allotments and farms to sell on. Each black-market sale, the government claimed, weakened the war effort and, as such, the judicial system came down heavily on the more persistent or larger operations.

With the services expanding rapidly the demand for food and forage also increased. The army depended upon a large number of civilian contractors for many things, amongst them were forage supplies. The increase in business meant that large profits could be made and opened up temptation. One of the leading forage suppliers was John Sloan Larmour (57) but at the start of the year very serious allegations were made against Mr Larmour, accusing him of being involved in a systemic pattern of bribery of army officers in various quartermaster positions in order to secure himself contracts. Mr Larmour seems to have been from a rather prominent family with their roots in Ireland and was in a position of some influence.

One of the first to be tried was not in fact the ringleader but one of his family. On 25 July 1941, a family member, one Jean Larmour of Ballycarrickmaddy, Lisburn, was tried at Belfast and was found guilty of having bribed a number of army officers to the sum of £500. Her counsel pleaded that she was not the ringleader of the scheme and did not realise the seriousness of her offences and asked the bench to show leniency. However, Lord Justice Barington said that he had a duty to the public in this matter and deplored the pollution of the army's standards in this manner and sentenced her to six months' imprisonment (without hard labour). Upon hearing the sentence Larmour collapsed in the dock and had to be carried away screaming.

In the summer of 1941 Mr Larmour was tried for giving bribes to the sum of £1,748 (over £89,797 today) to various people, many of them members of the army. The High Court at Edinburgh heard how the bribes had been paid to civilian clerks working for the army or to officers and men working as quartermasters in order to obtain official War Department contracts and that the crimes had been taking place for several years, extending back to twelve years before the war, but that Mr Larmour had not even ceased this practice when the country was facing its most serious crisis in 1940. The Advocate-Depute, Mr R. Sherwood Calver, said that 'one would have expected even the unscrupulous contractor to develop, however belatedly, a sense of decency' during wartime and stated that the crimes had amounted to a systematic attempt to corrupt those to whom the bribes were paid and 'to seduce them from their public duty'.[30] As a major contractor, Mr Larmour's scheme had not been confined to Scotland but had extended to England and Northern Ireland. Mr Calver declared that they had discovered that bribes had run from just £5 to as much as £449 and the majority had been paid to obtain information which should have been withheld in order for him to obtain contracts (in many cases the sums which rivals were bidding for contracts). A breakdown of the payments showed that payments had been made in Edinburgh, Belfast, Glasgow, Perth and South Queensferry and that the sums included £449 (over £23,000 today) to a man in Belfast, £215 (over £11,000) to an army officer in Edinburgh, £138 (over £7,000) to an Edinburgh clerk, and sums from £182 down to £5 to various members of the forces.

Defending Mr Larmour, Mr D.P. Blades appeared shocked by the vehemence of the prosecution's tone and said that if he had known of it in advance he would never have advised his client to plead guilty. In defending his client he attempted to portray Mr Larmour as both a loyal, patriotic expert and a businessman who had been simply a victim of corruption that, he alleged, was rife within the contracts system of the army. He told how Mr Larmour had enlisted in the Royal Army Service Corps (RASC) aged just 18 and had served in the army for nine years before being placed upon the reserve list. Once he had left the army he had put his knowledge of the contracts system to good use and had started his own business as a contractor, supplying the army with forage, sanitary services and hospital supplies. Mr Larmour had, according to his defence, performed excellent service during this time and had even received a commendation from the War Office (it would seem that Mr Larmour did not serve during the First World War even though he would have been only 30 at its outbreak; presumably his services as a contractor allowed him to avoid being recalled).

In summing up, Mr Blades once again tried to portray his client as an innocent caught up in a nefarious scheme which was not of his own concoction saying that Mr Larmour was 'more the victim of circumstances … than anything in the nature of a seducer' and argued that the matter of the illegally obtained contracts could surely be settled by the imposition of a fine rather than any custodial sentence as this would allow Mr Larmour to 'carry on the public work which is of the utmost importance at the present time'.[31]

Thanks to the thoroughness of the police investigation into Mr Larmour the case had several sequels which rumbled on for the next year. Two months after Mr Larmour had been imprisoned, fifteen people, including army officers, appeared privately in Edinburgh's Sheriff's Court charged with contravening the Prevention of Corruption Act in connection with bribes paid by Mr Larmour. A number of the army personnel were accused under the Official Secrets Act. This was because much of the information that had been passed to Mr Larmour involved details not only about army contracts but also details of camp locations and movements as well as coastal defences.

Mr Blades also stated that in committing these offences his client had lost his gratuity, pension rights and had brought disgrace upon his family. He added, rather unrealistically, that Mr Addison had not realised the seriousness of what he had done as he believed at the time that the information was not vital.

On the same day Private Vincent O'Connor (28) was sent to prison for six months after he had admitting accepting bribes (amounting to over £11) from Mr Larmour to remove tenders for army contracts from mail which he was duty-bound to collect from the Post Office. He was acting as a mail orderly and messenger, so that Mr Larmour could open them and read them before they were delivered to army HQ. The court heard how Private O'Connor had served in the Black Watch between 1931 and 1938 and had been recalled at the start of the war. The sheriff said that he had to take the matter very seriously but he realised that O'Connor was the tool of others in the matter and that he had gotten himself 'mixed up in an ugly and very dirty business'.[32]

Just three days later another related case was heard. This case highlighted how a criminal conspiracy could grow once one man had become involved in the crime. The trial was that of a War Office clerk, William John Ross (39), who had admitted to accepting payments amounting to over £138 from Larmour in exchange for information regarding army tenders and work done at army camps. Once again letters had been found in the possession of Larmour which confirmed the accused's complicity. Ross' defence explained in some detail how his client had become involved with Larmour when he had been introduced by a friend who was already accepting money from him (this was one of the men previously sentenced). On this first occasion, Larmour took the two men to lunch at a hotel and at the end of the lunch slipped a 10s note into Ross' hand. Ross asked his friend why he had done this and was told that Larmour often gave the clerks money for a drink. In the course of his duties and in subsequent meetings with Larmour, Ross quickly realised that Larmour had access to information regarding contracts and camps which even he did not know. By the time he had begun relaying information to Larmour he explained that his client had already accepted quite a lot of money and that he 'felt under an obligation'.[33]

On 28 October three more cases were heard in relation to the Larmour case. Two clerks who had, in the past, been employed by the RASC, John Ferrie (41) and Edward Morris (47), admitted contravention of the Official Secrets Act and the Prevention of Corruption Act and were sentenced to two years' imprisonment each.

Ferrie was a married man with four children but had given Larmour information about tenders, contracts, camps and movement of troops and had been paid over £182 (nearly £9,350) as, he told the court, he had been badly in need of money following a spell of unemployment during the war. Once again, Ferrie had been drawn in by an associate who was already involved. Morris, who was at the time working for the NAAFI had admitted to accepting over £126 (almost £6,500) between 1938 and 1940. This had been in exchange for communicating to Larmour the details of troop movements, lists of contractors applying for tenders and copies of letters from Scottish Command. He also admitted that he had failed to send tenders out to some firms and had suggested to Larmour what bids might be successful. Morris had served in the army for 21 years and had retired as a Warrant Officer in 1935. His solicitor said in mitigation that his client had spent much of the money on drink, that Larmour had always been free with his money (even when not receiving information), that since Morris' employment in the NAAFI at the start of the war, he had been unable to provide any useful information and that the breaches of the Official Secrets Act had been committed before the war began.

The third case was that of Lieutenant Joseph William Partridge, Royal Artillery, who appeared before the court in uniform, wearing a medal ribbon from the First World War. Partridge admitted contravention of the Prevention of Corruption Act. Partridge (45) had joined the RASC in 1937 as a corporal after service in the army of twenty-three years (he was transferred to the Royal Artillery and commissioned in May 1941) and between 1937 and 1938 had received just over £85 (almost £4,340) from Larmour for giving him information, obtaining army contracts and for ensuring that contracts for the army only went to Larmour. Sheriff Principal Brown felt some pity for Partridge, who had applied for transfer to the Royal Artillery as he was worried about his previous contact with Larmour, given his previous service, and said that he was treating the case as 'only fairly bad and not very bad' and sentenced him to nine months' imprisonment.

The case was an incredibly serious one, with the country still struggling to bring in necessary supplies and with the army on the defensive, it is no surprise that the plea of being a victim would not find much sympathy either in society or the establishment. With the defendant having pleaded guilty to the bribery charges and with the strong suspicions that, perhaps, the matter was even more serious than the trial had allowed for, Lord Stevenson imposed a sentence of three years penal servitude upon Mr Larmour.

In December the case had spread its tendrils to London and a Lieutenant Gerald Patrick Walsh (33), Royal Army Service Corps, was summonsed before West London Police Court accused of having accepted bribes amounting to £3 from Edinburgh based Mr Larmour when he was a Corporal in the RASC in 1938. At this time Walsh (33) had been employed as a clerk at Kensington Barracks where he had access to information on army forage supplies. When Larmour's property in Edinburgh was searched, the police found 140 letters from Walsh which made it obvious that he had been receiving money from Larmour since 1930. It was a familiar tale, with the young soldier accepting payments and then feeling that he was in Larmour's power and unable to resist further demands. In 1933 Walsh had an attack of conscience and went to the police where he made a full confession. Upon hearing this (the sources do not say how) Larmour called Walsh before him and 'threatened him with the direct penalties' whereupon Walsh was intimidated and tore up the confession in front of Larmour. Mr Larmour later apparently pasted the confession together as it was found during the police search. Walsh pleaded guilty to the charge and admitted that all in all he had accepted bribes of £40-£50 but that since the outbreak of war when he was commissioned he had refused to accept any further bribes from Larmour.[34]

The case demonstrated how the war offered potentially huge profits for those who were corrupt enough to break the laws governing the supply of food and forage.

Chapter 4

Food, Morale and Society in Wartime Britain

Many rural communities attempted to maintain a semblance of normality in the build up to the war by continuing to hold their annual agricultural shows. Just the week before the war began one of the most popular North Northumberland shows was held. Glendale Show was (and continues to be) extremely popular and a feature in the rural calendar of Northumberland. Held at Wooler the show attracted a crowd of thousands and, in the circumstances, this turnout was described as 'a distinct triumph'.[1] All classes were described as being of a very high quality with the best sheep and horses from both sides of the Border being on display. Highlighting the situation, however, was the presence of a stand representing the Women's Land Army which was offering advice and actively recruiting under the leadership of Mrs J.G.G. Rea of Berrington. Amongst the greatest winners in the sheep classes was well-known Northumbrian farmer Mr C.I.C. Bosanquet of Rock who won several prizes including the championship cup and the silver medal presented on behalf of the Society of Border Leicester Sheep Breeders; the small village of Rock was exceptionally successful with several farmers from the area winning prizes while others who were successful included Mr E. Cuthbert, Jun. of Brinkburn New Houses in Coquetdale. The horticultural and industrial classes were also a success as was the extensive equestrian and sporting programme. Notable visitors to the show included Sir Cuthbert Headlam (who was prospective Conservative candidate for Berwick), Captain, the Hon. Claud

Lambton, Major J.G.G. Rea, Captain A.L. Goodson and notable blackface sheep breeder Mr Arthur Cayley of Carham.

Across the north of the county, various leek shows, produce shows, whist drives and dances were taking place with attendances being maintained and people anxious to maintain as normal a life as possible. In Rothbury the second annual show of the Rothbury British Legion Horticultural Society was held at Grieves Hall. Once again there was a good attendance and the displays were of a very high quality. The show was opened by Lord and Lady Armstrong (introduced by Dr Reginald Armstrong). The most outstanding display of the show was Mr J. Atkin of Harle's open border flowers including a beautiful display of gladioli whilst the vegetable classes were also very fine. Elsewhere garden fetes were held in small communities across the area such as that in aid of the Eglingham and Old Bewick Churches which was held, with the permission of Colonel Henry Roland Milvain, in the grounds of Eglingham Hall.

As in many other farming communities local agricultural societies played a significant role in maintaining the morale of farmers while also undertaking fund raising campaigns for the more general war effort. On the last day of January 1943 Orkney Agricultural Society held its annual bull show at Kirkwall Auction Mart. The entry of forty Aberdeen Angus bulls was supposedly the best that had ever been seen at the event and the championship was won by Mr A. Calder of Sebay, St. Andrews, with a fifteen-month-old bull named Agrippa Sebay. The reserve champion was the patriotically named thirteen-month old bull Defiance of Midhouse, owned by Mr M. Horne of Midhouse, Evie. At the sale, Agrippa Sebay was sold to a Shapinsay farmer for 81 guineas and the reserve champion fetched 91 guineas. Two other bulls fetched more than the champion, one of these was a prize winner and the other one was an also-ran. The show, despite the wartime conditions, attracted a large crowd of farmers drawn from the east and west of the Scottish mainland along with those from the islands. Mr David Flett, the auctioneer, was very pleased with the results of the auction with high prices being met for all of the bulls which were sold.

We have already seen some examples of how rural communities and farming groups rallied around the wider war effort in addition to their traditional roles in the production of food. The enthusiasm for Spitfire Funds was almost universal. On Orkney this was reflected in the number of people who quickly stated they would contribute. These included James McDonald, a butcher from Albert Street in Kirkwall, who promised that he and other members of his family were willing and ready to contribute £100 to the fund. On 15 August 1940 the West Mainland Agricultural Society had a meeting at Dounby at which it was decided to hold sheepdog trials in aid of the, as yet to be formed, Orkney Spitfire Fund. The secretary of the society, Mr James Wood of Garson, Sandwick, told the newspaper that the support for the project was unanimous and that while they sincerely hoped that the fund would become a reality he did not know when the funds would be donated to various war charities. Mr Wood said that the show would mean 'Southerners will discover what the people of Orkney have long realised, that as a form of outdoor entertainment sheepdog trials have few equals' but that the most important consideration would be 'that all who support the event will be helping the RAF to blow Hitler's bombers out of the sky'.[2] The newspaper even made the suggestion that the society itself might put themselves forward as organisers of the fund.

The ploughing competitions which we have already seen continued in 1943 with the annual hedgelaying and ploughing competitions. Locally organised across the country by a combination of local agricultural societies they were increasingly helped by the local War Ag whose members recognised the opportunity to not only boost morale but also to disseminate good practice. The particularly well-organised Northumberland War Ag was one of the first to get involved. The Northumberland War Ag organised a hedgelaying and ploughing competition in October 1943, held at Thropton Demesne Farm. The competition attracted a large crowd and numerous competitors. The War Ag chair, Major Rea, used the opportunity to give a lecture on the work done by the War Ag and the plans for the future. There were three classes in the competition (ploughing with horse, ploughing with tractor and hedgelaying). Competitions like these took place across Britain and were a great boost to the morale of the rural community but also served a function in educating farmers on new techniques and technologies.

The case of Betty Reid, the Scottish agricultural student who had found some fame for winning ploughing competitions as a member for the WLA, was not an isolated one and ploughing seems to have been an activity into which many land girls threw themselves with both determination and skill. The wartime press covered many stories of land girls triumphing in ploughing competition up and down the country. In December 1944, for example, the *Northampton Mercury* carried an account of a ploughing competition organised by the Northamptonshire War Ag. The winner of the three-furrow category and overall match winner was a Miss R. Gilby.

Grumbles about the ration were particularly vociferous when people thought that the standard of staple foods was being reduced unfairly. In South Shields, County Durham, there was some dismay over food quality, with several letters appearing in the local press bemoaning the quality and price of staples such as bacon and sausage. At the end of January 1940 one anonymous correspondent wrote to the *Sunderland Echo and Shipping Gazette* stating that the reason the bacon ration had been increased was because working families had replaced it with sausage due to the price. The price of sausage had indeed increased from 3½d per lb in pre-war days to 10d per lb at the time of writing. The letter-writer complained that this could not be down to the price of meat as the wartime sausages contained so little. He described the wartime sausage as being a 'long string of mystery and bread'.[3] Instead, he believed that with workers being asked to refrain from asking for pay rises it was time that the retailers were also made to keep their prices down by order of the local food committees.

Another burden placed upon the housewife was the constant admonishments and encouragement to ensure that as little food was wasted as possible. Throughout the war housewives were urged to make the best use of what was available and numerous lectures were given to members of various organisations. The WI and the WVS were often at the forefront of these efforts but they were significantly backed by the MoF, who spent fortunes on various pamphlets and guides advising the housewife.

Salvage campaigns for metal, particularly aluminium, had seen housewives urged to give up their old pots and pans for the war effort. Amongst the more unusual items which people were encouraged to salvage, however, were bones from meat cuts. Housewives were told to wash the bones and leave them out to be collected in bundles. The bones were boiled down to make glue for the aircraft industry, ground up for fertiliser to return to the land or made into glycerine for high explosive bombs and shells. Adverts, for example, informed the doubtful that the 2oz bone from a chop could be used to make an explosive charge which could be used to fire two bullets from a Hurricane or Spitfire machine gun.

Alongside the velvet glove of encouragement was the steely threat of prosecution for those who deliberately wasted vital foodstuffs. In January 1943, for example, Miss Mary Bridget O'Sullivan of Normandy Avenue, Barnet, Herts, was fined the sum of £10 plus 2 guineas costs for instructing her maid to feed the birds on a daily basis. Her servant, Miss Domenica Rosa Persi, had been seen on two occasions throwing stale bread to the birds. When Miss O'Sullivan was interviewed by the local food enforcement officer, she admitted that the bread was put out every morning and stated that she could not see the birds starve and that she 'must continue to do it'. Her unfortunate maid was also found guilty and fined the sum of 5s for wasting the bread.[4]

For those who had the time to attend lectures held by various voluntary groups, a huge number of useful hints and tips were provided which encouraged attendees to preserve precious foodstuffs. The August 1940 meeting of the St Ola branch of the Women's Royal Institute (WRI), for example, had the subject of vegetable cooking as its main theme. The president read a paper containing many useful hints for cooking with vegetables and Mrs Harcus of Glaitness Farm presented her recipe for vegetable pie. Other subjects discussed during the meeting included the collection of garden flowers and a competition was held for the best arrangement, which was won by Mrs Twatt. The meeting, held at Kirkwall Grammar School, also featured a delicious tea for the many attendees and collections of socks, hospital cushions, bags and paper were handed in.

Among the tips which bombarded the British people was advice to preserve eggs for a little longer by rubbing the shells with lard (which sealed the pores) or by pickling them. Pork or lamb chops could be preserved by cooking them and then by storing them in a crock completely covered by fat.

The humble carrot was one vegetable which was not in shortage. The carrot, easy to grow and to store, was one vegetable which the public were encouraged to grow themselves. The government had, earlier in the war, run campaigns extolling the benefits from carrot consumption and many newspapers carried wartime recipes utilising the humble carrot. The public were even told that consumption of carrots improved night vision (crucial during the blackout), this was even given as a reason for the success of RAF night fighter pilots to draw attention away from Top Secret airborne radar, but they were also encouraged to eat the vegetable due to its health benefits. The night-fighter story partially came about from a military subterfuge. In the gloom-ridden days of early 1941, the press were allowed almost unprecedented access to Britain's leading night-fighter pilot, Wing Commander John Cunningham. The night-fighters relied, to a large extent, on radar interception gear but the authorities did not want this reported and instead it was stated that Cunningham had such good eyesight that his night vision was the equivalent to that of a cat, giving him the nickname Cats' Eyes Cunningham. The story was made more credible by the addition of a line saying that his night vision was maintained by a diet of carrots. The cartoon character Dr Carrot had already proven popular, but an entire carrot family was designed by a Disney cartoonist in the USA for use in the MoF campaigns. They included: Carroty George; Clara Carrot; and Pop

Carrot. Housewives were encouraged to experiment with carrot jam, curried carrot and even 'Carrolade' (a home-made juice made from carrots and swedes).

Potatoes and carrots were both cooked with the skin on to preserve nutrients and reduce wastage although those with pigs or chickens did often continue to peel some vegetables for feed. The MoF's Potato Pete comic character even acquired his own song on the subject. It went:

Those who have the will to win,
Cook potatoes in their skin,
Knowing that the sight of peelings,
Deeply hurts Lord Woolton's feelings.[5]

The MoF, under Woolton, was prepared to spend vast sums of money on propaganda campaigns aimed at convincing people to toe the line when it came to food. Some of its efforts were extremely helpful, such as the advice given to gardeners and those attempting to rear pigs or poultry for the first time, while others were rather less successful and came across as patronising in the extreme.

One of the more successful campaigns included the '*Kitchen Front*' broadcasts on the BBC. Aired six days of the week from 8:15 to 8:20 a.m., the show, aimed at housewives, consisted of advice on rationing; which foods were plentiful, which were scarce, how to avoid falling afoul of the multitude of new regulations, and so on. The show featured a variety of speakers but the main presenter was travel writer S.P.B. Mais. Among the more popular presenters was Dr Charles Hill, known as the radio doctor, who gave talks on how to prepare nutritious meals and advice on how to remain healthy on a wartime diet. Perhaps the most popular presenters, however, were the music-hall comediennes Elsie and Doris Waters. The sisters were approached and interviewed by non-other than Lord Woolton himself and, despite initial scepticism, Lord Woolton was impressed by their talents during the brief interview. The two quickly adopted the personas of two sisters, Gert and Daisy. The two characters presented a series of shows covering a wide variety of topics in a humorous fashion which found widespread favour. Comedy was a feature of the show throughout its run, even if some of it was rather forced and patronising.

During the spring of 1941 the series proved its worth. This was one of the worst periods of the war in terms of rationing and shortages so the programmes attempted to demonstrate useful alternatives to unavailable foods and maintain morale at the same time. One episode of the show instructed on preparing a meatless Sunday lunch and throughout the next week topics included: making marmalade from carrots; preserving eggs using various methods; trip showing behind the scenes at a Food Office; the use of plums; and a visit to one of the new works canteens. On the following Saturday, the show covered the difficulties faced by women workers who found themselves unable to get to the shops. In the following week a female doctor faced the unenviable and difficult task of demonstrating that many of the foods which people were most used to were not truly essential to their well-being. She explained how meat and dairy products could be replaced with vegetables and how wholemeal bread (a constantly contentious issue) was protective. Butter, she explained (largely in vain) was now redundant given that vitamins were being added to the more easily available margarine. Other broadcasts that month gave a variety of recipes using food which was off-ration. Offal featured heavily with recipes for giblet and liver sandwiches alongside those using liver and kidney. Vegetable soups also featured alongside advice on how to use precious meat scraps in hashes. The traditional full English breakfast was also a victim of the war with one show advising people how to make a nourishing breakfast consisting of a Yorkshire pudding stuffed with potatoes and topped, perhaps, with a precious rasher of bacon. The show also advised people, despite their fears of invasion, to heed the call not to stockpile food. Clearly, during this difficult time the show played an important role in allaying fears, while at the same time offering very valuable advice at a time of great hardship.

Many of the recipes issued through the 'Kitchen Front' or official pamphlets were drawn up by MoF home economists. Many were for mock foods; mock goose, mock cream, etc. Others were formulated to address specific concerns, for example, making the fats ration last, which was a particular problem for many. Bread was widely available but the butter ration was small and some of the larger margarine ration had to be kept for use in baking. An MoF leaflet entitled 'Making the Fat Ration Go Further' gave an ingenious solution. It advised housewives to take 8 oz of butter or margarine and cream 6 oz with a spoon until it was softened. The remaining 2 oz were used in the making of a white sauce combining a tablespoon of flour, half a pint of milk and a pinch of salt. This was then cooled and mixed with the fat in a bowl shortly before use. Thus, the half a pound of spread was turned into almost double this amount.

Potato Pete, one of the many vegetable characters that the MoF used, urged Britons to combine melted margarine or butter with an equal amount of mashed potato and to use this as a spread. Many people turned to using the drippings from their precious meat ration to provide a sandwich spread, combining it with chutney, chopped leek or onion, herbs or vinegar. Housewives got used to rendering down every possible piece of meat for the fat it produced.

With sugar also rationed and in short supply, the great British 'cuppa' had to be enlivened through other means. Some had access to honey but this was often too precious to use simply to sweeten tea and so a great many Britons took to using saccharin for the first time. This was available from chemists, was not rationed and became largely accepted through lack of choice. For the MoF this was a mixed blessing as, although it saved precious sugar, saccharin has no nutritional value and so did not provide energy in the same way.

The plethora of wartime recipes intended to allow people to eat healthily without breaking the rationing system was a feature in almost every local newspaper. Many of the recipes were vetted or created by nutritionists working for either local authorities or the MoF. Mock dishes which sought to recreate the flavours of unavailable foods or ingredients in short supply were common. The *Belfast News-Letter* of 23 November 1940, for example, gave recipes for mock goose and mock crab on toast (see Appendix 1).

In August 1943, the *Belfast Telegraph* featured an innovative recipe for a mock veal and ham pie which used corned beef and tinned sausage as a substitute for the original ingredients. Like many other recipes which featured in the local press this one originated with a food production and retail company, in this case the producers of Stork Margarine. Indeed, so committed were they to producing new recipes using their product that they even had their own Stork Margarine Cookery Service which had produced the recipe and others in what was their 45th and 46th wartime cookery booklets, entitled *'Cold Meals for Hot Weather'* and *'Holidays at Home'*. The firm were keen to point out in their advert that all of their recipes had been approved by the MoF. Readers could obtain the booklet simply by cutting out and sending the appropriate coupon to the address listed.

The MoF, the WVS, the WI and a host of other local and national organisations organised demonstrations on cookery techniques throughout the war. These sought to offer alternatives to the hard-worked wartime housewife and also served the purpose of strengthening the war effort by ensuring that people thought about food more critically and more ingeniously. Many of these demonstrations were given by qualified home economists or nutritionists. They always put easily available ingredients at the forefront with vegetables and fruits the most common themes. So, for example, a typical example of these lectures took place at the Market Square in Lancaster on 5 January 1942 when Miss E.M. Taylor, MCA, lectured and gave a demonstration on the subject of 'Wartime Cookery'. The main features of the demonstration were the production of carrot marmalade, carrot chutney and bean cutlets.

At the end of the same month the carrot theme was continued in the local press with the MoF-invented character of Dr Carrot giving advice on how to use the ubiquitous vegetable. The *Manchester Evening News,* in a column entitled 'Dr Carrot at the breakfast table' was typical of this campaign. In it, Dr Carrot advised that carrot margarine was delicious and informed readers that the more carrots one ate the more stores of Vitamin A the body built up (see Appendix 1).

We have seen how pie recipes found great popularity with the thrifty housewife and how pies were supplied to rural workers and villagers. The humble pie underwent a transformation during the war as recipe after recipe appeared in newspapers, pamphlets and leaflets. *The Northern Whig & Belfast Post* writer Florence Irwin, writing under the pseudonym 'The Housewife', informed readers that a substantial pie was an exceptional standby in a wartime kitchen as it could be used for lunch or supper and to feed unexpected guests. She then went on to give a recipe for a cold chicken or rabbit pie which was both frugal and nutritious (see Appendix 1).

One problem with the numerous recommended pie dishes was the strict rationing of fats which were needed to make pastry. A variety of solutions were offered and during the spring of 1941, a time, as we have heard, of great shortage, the *Sussex Express and County Herald* offered advice on how to make shortcrust pastry in a wartime fashion, when the usual method of using half a pound of flour and a quarter pound of fat was clearly out of the question. Sour milk could be used, claimed the writer, with the added bonus that it made for wonderfully light pastry. To get around the fats problem, the housewife was advised to utilise meat dripping; beef dripping was the most useful for this, but mutton tended to make for hard pastry. One solution to this was to mix 2 oz of margarine with 1 oz of mutton dripping. For those families who could not spare any of their fats ration for baking pastry, the writer also provided a suet pastry recipe which required no margarine.

The same article also gave a recipe for a tasty dessert which was an alternative to a fruit pie with the bread being used as an alternative to pastry. This involved lining the bottom of a pie dish with stale bread before covering it with what fruits were available. The mix was sweetened by placing either a quarter pound of dates or a tablespoonful of syrup on top. A cup of water was added before the short pastry crust was placed on top and the 'pie' was baked in the usual manner before being served with custard, it was also possible to make the dessert with a suet pastry.

Thrift was the name of the game and housewives were exhorted to make use of any possible ingredient. The same article as that above was typical in offering several tips to the embattled housewife. One of these tips criticised many housewives for not making good use of the rich brown jelly which formed beneath meat dripping. The writer advised removing this jelly to use in gravy or in soups. A useful tip was to put a little water into a basin before pouring in fresh dripping. When the dripping was removed, any moisture underneath it could be scraped off and the dripping could be melted down again so that it could be poured into a jar and the resultant rich gravy could be used.

Other thrifty dishes which were encouraged to make the most of any scraps and easily available ingredients included various types of rissole. The corned beef rissole became a commonplace dish but other ingredients were also provided with rissole recipes. In 1940, the *Taunton Courier and Western Advertiser* gave advice on how to utilise the most unappetising leftovers from a joint of beef. The popularity of such waste-not dishes was maintained. Three years later the *Western Daily Press* featured a recipe for savoury rissoles using vegetables (see Appendix 1).

Given the huge emphasis placed upon the consumption of vegetables during the war (they were not rationed and conveniently grown at home) it is no surprise that a huge number of the recipes presented in newspapers involved the use of them. Typical of the wartime vegetable recipes was the infamous Woolton Pie which came to be either loved or hated by many in wartime Britain but there were myriad other recipes which utilised a mixture of vegetables. Several of these recipes combined vegetables with the generally disliked but easily obtainable national loaf (see Appendix 1). The constant barrage of propaganda assured the British people that vegetables were nourishing and provided much needed vitamins.

Another key aim of the rationing policy was to ensure that there would be no need for food queues. The authorities viewed food queues as anathema, and in 1941 the phenomenon of queuing was described as being 'a bigger menace to public morale than several serious German air raids'.[6] In this respect, the policy was an utter failure, as queues became part of wartime life for the majority. Queues, not only for food but for commodities such as stockings, were being described as commonplace in most areas from the first months of 1941.[7] Queues were most prevalent in what official reports described as the 'working-class areas' as people attempted to obtain meagre supplies and to 'make the coupons stretch as far as [they] could'. It was common for people to travel a considerable distance to queue for hours at a time. One woman, then a young girl, remembered being sent by her mother several miles out of her town to a neighbouring town to try to obtain cooking fats.[8] Such queues in working class areas were sometimes a partial result of the thriftiness that had been encouraged by the government in that some queues formed when people tried to obtain supplies for baking to make sure that food supplies went further.

In the spirit of making do and adapting, keen bakers (and there were many) found new sources of baking ingredients. In North Shields, for example, people even queued outside a tripe factory to obtain cooking fat.[9] Others ensured that the fat from their meat ration was not wasted and rendered it down along with fat from other sources such as tins of corned beef.

The determination to make the best of what was available led, as we have seen, to some fairly ingenious recipes and this spirit continued right to the end of the war (and, indeed, beyond). In the fourth year of the war, with rationing and the effects of the Battle of the Atlantic being felt very badly, Aberdeen housewives, for example, were attempting to find ever-more ingenious methods of providing tasty and nutritious food for their families. Providing sweet courses was a particularly knotty problem but the local press ran semi-regular articles on cooking alongside short recipes. In early March, for example, a recipe for Spice Pie appeared alongside claims that the recipe was tasty, unusual, did not require a lot of sugar and, crucially, did not take a great deal of time to prepare (see Appendix 1).

By 1942, however, the period prior to Christmas was marked by widespread discontent centred on the frequent shortages and the Ministry of Information (MoI) registered complaints from eleven regions. On Tyneside, the Christmas of 1942 appears to have passed quietly, however, with little mention of any major dissatisfaction aside from the shortages of alcohol that were provoking strong criticism at the time.[10] In a national sense the two final Christmases of the war continued this established pattern of pre-holiday grumbling followed by a reasonably successful celebration. The most consistent grumbles were always over the shortage of alcohol and the price and availability of poultry.

Christmas, as we have seen, was always a particularly trying time for those attempting to provide not only a nourishing meal but one which recreated some of the pre-war festivities. Rationing and shortages of course affected people on a daily basis but there was particular concern from the authorities that shortages during national holiday periods could affect morale particularly badly. The approach to the wartime Christmases was always a time of tension for those who were responsible for providing for a family as the gathering of sufficient supplies for the holiday period was acutely problematic. No other period provided so many inconveniences, or provoked so much determination to maintain a cheerful atmosphere. The majority of people were determined to have as ordinary a Christmas as possible. The period before Christmas was stressful as last minute efforts ensued to acquire the necessary foodstuffs and queues tended to be larger despite the often poor weather. Grumbling over high prices and scarcity of goods was commonplace but the first few Christmases of the war appeared to be a success, with most people being able to acquire supplies of food and looking on the situation as being a necessary sacrifice.

The festivities over the first few wartime Christmases were described as being as normal as possible despite the public being upset at shortages of meat, eggs and onions and the prices of Christmas fowl being described as 'exorbitant'; a common complaint echoed across the land.[11] By 1942, however, the period prior to Christmas was marked by widespread discontent centred on the frequent shortages and the Ministry of Information (MoI) registered complaints from eleven regions. On Tyneside, the Christmas of 1942 appears to have passed quietly, however, with little mention of any major dissatisfaction aside from the shortages of alcohol that were provoking strong criticism at the time.[12]

Trying to provide not only a nourishing meal but one which recreated some of the pre-war festivities of Christmas remained a problem. For those who were struggling, or for the many service personnel based in towns and cities across Britain, the British Restaurants and other canteens were a godsend. In 1943 one Edinburgh local wrote an account of his Christmas morning in Edinburgh and the surrounding villages. He described how he had gotten up while it was still dark and breakfasted on a traditional Full English breakfast complete with black pudding before setting out. During his journey he was walking through Gorgie and decided to visit Dalry House only to find that the ground floor was now being used as a British Restaurant (named 'Fare Ye Weel'). After partaking of a cup of coffee and chocolate biscuit at the restaurant he set out once more into the city where he took a bus to Princes Street. Later he followed one group of Polish soldiers into a Rest House in Waterloo Place where he found men and women of a wide variety of the services, including 'a black man in uniform', at a long bar. The servicemen and women were able to purchase a Christmas lunch of soup and then turkey, followed by Christmas pudding for the sum of just 1s. After returning home the writer enjoyed his own Christmas repast of dinner with 'a good fowle', fruit pudding and sauce and 'other comforts'.

The government was well aware that Christmas was a time in which many people tried to make their rations stretch further and to include a few luxuries so they attempted to alleviate the problem, to some extent, in 1944. With Christmas looming there was a shred of good news as it was announced that rationing on biscuits and beans was to be reduced. The points cost of most types of biscuits was to be halved while on some cans and packs of beans it was reduced by more than half. However, the authorities cautioned people that although supplies of biscuits would be increased they might not reach the shops before the festive period.

From 1942 offal went on ration, with sausages following at the start of 1943 (they were both removed from the list in 1945), but there were shortages of some type of offal, while the wartime sausages were a constant cause for complaint due to the small amount of meat in them. As a result of these complaints the MoF passed a regulation that any sausage had to contain at least 10 per cent meat.

Once sausages where placed on the ration list the government cracked down to ensure that they were nourishing and nutritious. Increasingly, soya bean was used to bulk out the new wartime sausages (a move largely welcomed as it resulted in less bread being used) and the sausages, as a result, became both firmer and meatier. As a result, many newspapers ran recipes with which the housewife could use the sausages to provide substantial meals. The *Dundee Evening Telegraph*, for example, ran an article on 31 May 1943 which gave several such recipes, including for Pembrokeshire Pudding, Cabbage and Sausage Scramble, and Meat Roll (see Appendix 1).

Tinned sausage meat from the USA proved very popular, this was true year-round but especially at Christmas. The large tubs of sausage meat from Wilson's Mor, in particular. Even though it cost sixteen points it provided enough meat for several meals and also came with the added bonus of having approximately ½ lb of fat on top which could be re-used by the thrifty cook.

Unusual Foods

Ensuring that there was an adequate supply of food was only one of the MoF's duties. It was also essential to morale that the British people felt reasonably content with both the supply of food and what foods were available to them. In addition to the standard food ingredients, the MoF was responsible for the introduction of a variety of so-called welfare foods. This was largely a part of Woolton and Drummond's plans to improve the health of poor children and mothers. Despite the decrease in supplies there was a great emphasis placed upon ensuring adequate supplies of milk were allocated to vulnerable groups such as children, nursing mothers and mothers-to-be (who were also given extra meat rations). Two varieties of dried, powdered milk were introduced. National Dried Milk was a baby food while Household Milk was for general consumption and was dried skimmed milk. Thus, infants under the age of 5 and expectant mothers received one pint per day of milk while schoolchildren received a third of a pint (a popular scheme which was only revoked in 1971 by Margaret Thatcher, Secretary of State for Education and Science).

With the shortages, people in Britain had to adapt their palates to a variety of unusual foods. One of the most despised was whale meat. Said by many to be tough and tasting of fish no matter how it was prepared it offended many a Briton when presented as a steak. By 1940 a number of articles appeared in the press claiming that the British troops on the Faroe Isles were existing largely on a diet of whale meat.

Housewives were advised to consider using unrationed sheep heads to make brawn or sheep's head stew (a staple in the not so distant past in parts of Scotland and the Borders). Those living near reservoirs could fish for eels or minnows and other small fish. A variety of bird's eggs could be harvested and used, either in cooking or baking. The author's father remembers collecting gulls eggs when he and his siblings were evacuated to Alston in Cumberland. In Scotland, people were advised on the ways in which the fishy and salty taste could be removed from the flesh of cormorants. The advised technique was to submerge the flesh in the sea for a whole day. Other methods included burying the flesh in mossy ground. One man writing to the press said that he had eaten both boiled and roasted cormorant. The eggs could also be used in baking.

Consumption of horseflesh increased during the war despite the traditional British resistance to this form of sustenance while corned beef (much of it from Argentina) found favour with many using it to make hashes, rissoles or fritters, amongst other meals. Other tinned meat products were brought in from America. A variety of these were available, including Mor, Prem and Tang but the most favoured, most famous and most widely available was Spam. Overcoming initial resistance the British people took remarkably well to Spam, made with pork shoulder and ham, and its popularity has continued ever since.

The British had always maintained an abhorrence of eating horse meat but the war saw necessity overtake this resistance (although the majority still remained reluctant). While horse meat was not rationed and despite the initial reluctance, queues formed for the meat as desperation overcame doubt in many minds. Horses bought for human consumption were always supposed to be bought alive for slaughter, with prices in 1941 ranging from £5–20. There were, however, repeated claims that inferior quality meat was finding its way into the human food chain. In November 1941, for example, a Yorkshire firm which bought horses for human consumption wrote to the press to deny claims that a dead horse on a Cornwall farm had been bought for just 5s. Horse meat was also used for dog and cat food and the firm pointed out that this knackers' meat had never been bought for less than 15s and was sold at the controlled price of 8d/lb.

Undoubtedly there were those who saw the opportunity for illegal profit in horse flesh. In 1942, the worst year of the war for many shortages, there were a large number of prosecutions for such offences. On 12 June, for example, Millicent Lowe of 146 Broad Street, Hanley, Staffs, was brought before the magistrates at Stoke. She was charged with having sold horse meat at a price exceeding that which was allowed. Found guilty, she was fined the sum of 5s while an accomplice, Mr Leslie Howard Foster, was fined £5 with an additional £2 2s costs.

One of the main ways in which criminals made a profit from the sale of horse meat was by illegally selling meat which was not fit for human consumption. In order to try to stop this the MoF ordered that all such meat had to have a dye injected into it which turned the meat green. Just days after the case stated above, the magistrates at Plympton fined a licensed slaughterman, Frederick Reeves of Yolland Road, Ugborough, the sum of a guinea with £1 17s 8d in costs. The MoF testified that on 28 May 3 cwt of horse meat which had been judged unfit for human consumption was observed being delivered to a pet shop in Torquay. The MoF inspector found that the meat had not been dyed. After tracing the consignment to Mr Reeves the inspector questioned him and was told that he had run out of dye and had been unable to obtain any more.

Those wishing to sell horse meat for human consumption had to obtain licences to do so from the MoF. In mid-September 1943, for example, a successful application was made for such a licence by Mr E. Carlisle of 68 Saville Street, North Shields. It was explained that the application was for the transfer of a licence which had previously been granted to Greer Ltd of Sandyford Road in nearby Newcastle upon Tyne.

As rationing and the effects of the Battle of the Atlantic continued to severely restrict food supplies, the people of Scotland and elsewhere turned to recipes from traditional Scottish (and, indeed, northern English) cuisine to fill out their diets. Stovies made with corned beef (or any offcuts if these were available – which they often were not) always remained a firm favourite with the flavour being enhanced by the addition of the ubiquitous OXO cube. Potted haugh or heed (made from the lower leg or head of a sheep) was not always so welcome but was nourishing and ensured that the most was made out of any available protein. Soup was also made from the meat boiled from a sheep's head with a broken marrow bone added to improve the flavour. Tripe also continued to make its contribution to many a diet, as did haggis and various other offal dishes (including boiled cow's udder) while fish cakes provided some variety (although they often contained noticeably more potato than before the war) and Spam fritters were an almost ever-present. Families who kept livestock had a few more options available to them. Hens not only provided meat but, perhaps even more importantly, a steady supply of eggs which could be sold or bartered to neighbours and friends as well as being used by the family themselves.

As rationing was set to continue long after the war and with queues at fishmongers growing larger, the government looked for sources of supplies of tinned fish from the Empire. It believed it had found the answer with snoek (or snook). The relative of tuna and mackerel came from South Africa and from 1945 the tinned fish was easily available off ration. Some 11 million cans were shipped to Britain. Unfortunately, the people of Britain failed to appreciate the new product, with many calling it smelly, oily, foul-tasting and inedible. Despite MoF efforts to provide recipes for such delicacies as snoek paste or snoek piquant, there were a huge amount of tins left unsold at the end of the war and the government repackaged them as cat food.

Chapter 5

Communal Feeding and the British Restaurants

For those who could still afford to eat out, a wide selection of restaurants were still available in many cities, even though some had closed. Those that remained had been forced to pay lip service to the new situation of rationing. Nevertheless, entertainment could still be found hand-in-hand with food in some places. The New Queen's Brasserie which stood next to The Empire in Leicester Square was a very popular destination for many who found themselves in London in 1940. The maitre-de, Mr Cope, was famed for his smart appearance and wearing of a carnation. While many restaurants had been forced to close, the New Queen's had restricted its hours. Lunch time opening was cancelled but the restaurant still opened for dinner. A peppy review in *The Bystander* of 16 October bemoaned how a dinner break meal and stein of Dale's Cambridge Ale was no longer possible but went on to describe the convivial evening atmosphere, where dancing and music, provided by Java and his boys, was enjoyed by 'half the officers on leave in London'. The reviewer particularly praised the restaurant for its quality, informality and economy.

In affluent Mayfair, Shepherd's Tavern in the Market maintained its popularity. Hosted by Oscar, who had previously worked at the Monseigneur at the Berkeley, the prevailing atmosphere was one of relaxed conviviality. The reviewer said that air raid warnings did not seem to worry Oscar, his staff or his patrons, most of whom were in uniform. The many junior officers who thronged Shepherd's discovered that their rates of pay could still allow them to enjoy 'first-class but unpretentious food' such as 'the best sort of joint to such dishes as steak, grouse and mushroom pie' while the drinks were sold at prices comparable to those in public houses.[1]

An important piece of the plan to allow everyone to obtain sufficient nourishing food were the communal feeding centres which were set up in schools and churches where families could get a nourishing meal. The idea for the communal feeding centres, which would later become 'British Restaurants', came from Mrs Flora Solomon. Mrs Solomon was in charge of the staff canteens at Marks & Spencer. She was inspired by the work of the Londoners' Meal Service which London County Council had begun in September 1940 to feed Londoners who had been bombed out during the Blitz. It was fortunate that Mrs Solomon knew Lord Woolton personally and, after discussing her ideas with him, she was given permission to set up the scheme. After getting permission from Simon Marks, Mrs Solomon set up her first Communal Feeding Centre in Kensington using Marks & Spencer staff to run the centre.

Thus, the British Restaurants originated in the need to be able to provide cheap, nourishing food to those who had been bombed out during the Luftwaffe's campaign against Britain. Building on the experiences of the National Kitchens of the First World War and the setting up of emergency feeding centres under the control of either local authorities, ARP services or volunteer groups (notably the WVS), they were originally called Community Feeding Centres but were, allegedly, renamed on the instruction of Winston Churchill who appreciated the patriotic boost of the new name.

Organised by the MoF, British Restaurants were run by the local authorities or volunteers on a non-profit basis and aimed to supply healthy and nourishing (off-ration) meals for a maximum of 9d per serving (approximately £1 today). As the scheme developed cafés, schools and other buildings were taken over and mobile canteens and even a delivery service, called the Cash and Carry Restaurant, was organised in some areas. British Restaurants were a huge success and by 1943 there were 2,160 across the country, serving over 600,000 meals per day.

Local corporations were expected to organise schemes to shelter, feed and re-house those who had been either temporarily or permanently rendered homeless. Most came up with similar schemes although there were regional variations. This was a vast undertaking with local authorities having to prepare to house and feed possibly tens of thousands of people at extremely short notice and under very trying conditions.

In May 1940, for example, Newcastle City Council estimated that its system of rest and feeding centres could cope with approximately 14,000 people. On Tyneside, as elsewhere, authorities approached a variety of local businesses in an effort to secure more sites for use as emergency rest and feeding centres. Locations with canteen facilities were also sought out and requests were made as to whether they would be able to provide emergency feeding facilities. Many of the best canteens, however, were located within major industrial concerns and were fully occupied keeping workers fed throughout the day and night. Their locations also made them targets for any prospective bombing raid on their locality and so most of these concerns responded negatively. In Newcastle, however, several major department stores, notably Mark & Spencer, Fenwick and C & A Modes, responded to these requests in a very positive manner and were utilised as emergency feeding stations throughout the war, both for the homeless and for ARP workers.

The system was not perfect and inefficiencies caused by restrictions placed upon them by central government continued to plague the feeding centres. It was standard procedure to serve cold, tinned food when a feeding centre was opened. This food would then have to be paid for and replaced. An incident in September 1940, which left thirty Newcastle residents homeless, led to the discovery that it was cheaper to obtain a hot meal from a local central kitchen than it was to replace the tinned foods that were in storage. This became standard procedure where feasible in Newcastle but was not officially recognised by the central government.

In response to concerns raised by Lord Woolton regarding the physical deterioration of the populace due to poor nutrition, communal feeding centres were also created. These centres could purchase food more cheaply and provided a nourishing, if basic, menu, usually consisting of potatoes and vegetable pie (the much-despised Wooton Pie). The centres were immediately welcomed, especially in deprived areas, and the menus expanded slightly to provide cheap, yet nutritious, three-course meals. Winston Churchill was pleased by the development but, typically, wanted to inject his own patriotic style into the system and, at his urging, the centres were quickly renamed British Restaurants.

Most British Restaurants were run through the local corporation but this was often in conjunction with other partners. Many of the British Restaurants were opened by well established companies, with cinema companies seemingly especially keen. Amongst these, the Gaumont chain was one which was particularly enthusiastic. British Restaurants also provided a handy place for those dignitaries who were keen to show their patriotic virtues. In Coventry, at the end of April 1940, for example, Gaumont British Restaurant, next to Gaumont Palace, played host to the mayor and mayoress of Coventry when they welcomed their counterparts from Ramsgate,who were there to encourage the residents of Coventry to holiday at the resort, contrary to government guidelines.

1941 saw a boom in the opening of British Restaurants. Many local authorities were in intense competition with each other to obtain permission and equipment to launch British Restaurants in their own areas. In London there was particularly keen competition between different boroughs and areas and there was a rash of openings throughout the year. Willesden, for example, opened its first British Restaurant on 26 May at Percy Road in Kilburn. As was often the case the restaurant was officially opened with a lunch for local dignitaries and invited guests (often the day before the restaurant officially opened). In this case the restaurant was opened by the mayor, Alderman W.H. Ryde, and the guest of honour was the

Parliamentary Secretary to the MoF, Major Gwilym Lloyd George. The major congratulated the mayor and the council on the opening of the restaurant and on the quality of the meal.

The more affluent areas which had not at first been prioritised by the MoF began to also put in place plans for their own schemes and there were numerous restaurants opened throughout the summer and autumn. On 5 August, Chiswick opened its first British Restaurant at the Catholic Hall on Chiswick Common Road. On the day before the official opening the restaurant gave a preview to around 100 prominent residents. Amongst the gathered dignitaries were the mayors of Brentford and Chiswick, Acton and Ealing. Councillor K.A. Cleland, mayor of Brentford and Chiswick, praised the restaurant and congratulated the chair of the Food Committee, Councillor Hedley Fry. In his reply, Councillor Fry stated that the opening of this first restaurant was just the beginning and that a second restaurant was soon to open at St Paul's Hall, Brentford. Describing the repast that the gathering had just enjoyed (consisting of soup (2d), steak and kidney pie, potatoes and cabbage (8d) and custard or jam tart (2d), tea (1d), or bread (1d)) he said that it was a very inexpensive meal but that the usual fare would be a good dinner of soup, meat and two veg, bread and sweets for the sum of 1s 2d.

Councillor C. Dobbs, the Mayor of Acton, said that the true reason for the British Restaurants was to eliminate all waste, something which would be vital if shipping losses continued. The Mayor of Ealing, who was a native of Chiswick, commented that at the present time Ealing was concentrating on looking after the local children but had hopes of extending feeding facilities very soon.

In fact, Southall already had a British Restaurant. The Borough Café had been opened by the mayor (Alderman G. Smith) on 21 April. Based at St John's Church Mission Hall on Hartington Road, the café served lunches from 12–2 p.m. The meals consisted of meat and two veg and a pudding for the sum of 10d. The meals could be eaten either on the premises or could be taken away.

In contrast to Councillor Dobbs' warnings over future shortages the government was anxious to reassure the population of London that there were more than adequate food stores for the capital. The opening of a British Restaurant in Edmonton on 25 August 1941 offered the London Divisional Food Officer, Mr W.G. Kirby, the opportunity to make a statement supporting this claim. Mr Kirby told the assembly that food stocks in London were larger at this point than at any time in the past twelve months and went on to reassure Londoners that he had under his control not only the usual stocks but also stocks of the six most important commodities sufficient to provide rations and, in some cases, double rations for the entire population for a fortnight in case of emergency.

Most of those who worked at the British Restaurants were volunteers but some staff at some of the restaurants were salaried. At the end of August 1941 the new British Restaurant which was to be opened at Victoria Road in Ruislip Manor, Hillingdon, was advertising for several staff. The vacancies were for a cook/manageress (at £3-£3 10s), a cook (at £2 10s per week) and for kitchen hand-cleaners (at £1 10s per week). All of the staff would also be entitled to a free meal as part of their conditions of employment.

There were many reasons for setting up British Restaurants. Mostly it was to provide nutritious meals for those who might otherwise struggle but in at least one case it was to prevent squabbles between hosts and evacuated women. The village of Ramsbury in Wiltshire (population 1,500) had been relatively isolated from the war, never having heard a bomb, but it had played welcoming host to many evacuees from blitzed areas of London. As a result it had been decided to open a British Restaurant to provide meals primarily for these London evacuees. An official told the *Daily Mirror* that they were looking ahead and that the 'answer to the problem of properly feeding evacuees is to start communal feeding'. The same official also told the reporter that while there might be room for more evacuees it was expecting too much of a Ramsbury housewife to share her kitchen with a woman who had been evacuated with her family.

The official told the reporter that to 'expect two women to share one kitchen, and perhaps the cooking utensils, is asking a lot'.[2]

The British Restaurant scheme often benefited from celebrity and VIP patronage which boosted the popularity and acceptability of the restaurants. As we have seen, one enthusiastic group of sponsors for the British Restaurant scheme was the film industry. At the beginning of September 1941 the romantic comedy *Jeannie* came out in the cinemas. The star of the film was US-born actress Barbara Mullen.[3] Miss Mullen was a popular star and when *Jeannie* premiered at the Odeon in Bournemouth she made a personal appearance. Part of her visit included a tour of the town with the mayor and a visit to a local British Restaurant where a simple lunch was taken.

In mid-September, the chair of Ealing's British Restaurants and School Canteens Committee, Alderman F.F. Woodward, could announce that consultations with MoF representatives were ongoing but that permission had been granted for the establishment of several British Restaurants. The first was to be in a building which had been requisitioned as a feeding centre by the Billeting Committee earlier in the war. This initial British Restaurant was aiming to feed 3,000– 3,500 people daily. Part of its efforts would be preparing meals and shipping them out (in containers) to schools for some 1,500 children. The MoF officials had also recommended that the authority rent out four premises in the Northfields area. Two of these would become British Restaurants, one would be a kitchen and the other a store for food supplies for the restaurants. One of the restaurants was located in a block of shops between Northfields Station and The Plough.

On 22 September 1941, the Minister of Food, Lord Woolton, visited Slough, Buckinghamshire, to open what was said to be the 1,000th British Restaurant. In his speech Lord Woolton said that he hoped to go on with the scheme and open a total of at least 2,000 British Restaurants. He also had a word of warning for local authorities, telling them that in times of emergency they must be prepared to feed tenfold the amount of people that the British Restaurants were currently catering for and that this would be the case even if gas, water and electricity supplies were cut. He was also keen to point out that the British Restaurants allowed children to obtain nutritious meals even if both parents were working. In view of the dislocation to the lives of many children, Lord Woolton also took the opportunity to express the view that local authorities should create special canteens which would cater especially for the needs of growing children.

The local authority in Ealing was also anxious to expand its feeding capabilities when it came to feeding schoolchildren and anticipated Lord Woolton's advice. As a result, the chair of the Education Committee, Councillor T.P. May, informed his fellow councillors that from 22 September two new school canteens were to be opened at Coston School and Grange School. The canteens were going to start small, providing 50–60 meals every day but it was hoped that by the end of October the Coston site would be feeding 250 children every day.

They depended upon volunteers and so the opening hours varied from restaurant to restaurant. Some opened almost all day long while others opened only at lunchtimes. One of the latter examples was the British Restaurant which opened at 85 Uxbridge Road, Ealing, in November. The British Red Cross organised the restaurant, which was located at its local HQ and any profits went to the organisation. The volunteer staff who oversaw the restaurant worked three hour shifts with the restaurant being open from 12–2 p.m. every day offering 1s meals. The restaurant quickly proved hugely popular. Indeed, such was the success of the restaurant that there had been shortages for latecomers on the first few days. This had quickly been remedied when the organisers learned just how popular the restaurant was and an appeal went out for more volunteers.

Most British Restaurants were designed to be permanent (or at least wartime) affairs but there were incidents where emergency restaurants were also set up to aid a population which had met with the misfortune of heavy bombing. Following the devastating blitz on Coventry in November 1941, for example, Mrs Solomon, the woman who first conceived of what would become the British Restaurant scheme, used the staff from the bombed-out Marks & Spencer store to staff a communal feeding centre in the city.

The phenomenon of the British Restaurant continued to attract attention from all quarters. When the new US ambassador to Britain, John Gilbert Winant, arrived in March 1941 he had made himself immediately popular by distancing himself from his pro-appeasement predecessor, Joseph P. Kennedy Jnr, by stating that there was no place he would rather be than Britain. For some time it had been customary for the US ambassador to pay at least one visit to Plymouth where he would give a public speech. Winant visited the battered city in November. The usual location for the luncheon in his honour was the Assembly Room of the Royal Hotel but this was one of many buildings which had been damaged by enemy action and instead, no doubt in an effort to demonstrate patriotism and solidarity, the luncheon was held at a local British Restaurant where a simple wartime meal was enjoyed.

The British Restaurant in Slough which had become the 1,000th such establishment was visited in November 1941 by a journalist from the *Daily Herald*. The journalist began with a criticism of what he had apparently witnessed at other British Restaurants, saying that the establishments were not opened to 'attract the shiftless housewife who is too lazy to cook and too casual to shop'. Nor, he continued, were they 'intended to supplement the rations of the greedy'. Nor were they intended to be 'turned into profit making enterprises'. The British Restaurant idea was, he stated, sound, democratic and a common-sense idea and it must not be allowed to become perverted by what he euphemistically called 'the human element'.[4]

The opening of new British Restaurants continued to attract the attention of celebrities and politicians and photo opportunities to demonstrate a united front were commonplace. In January 1942, for example, farmworkers employed by David Lloyd George were treated to a meal at the British Restaurant in Haslemere. Pictures of the farmworkers toasting the politician were later published in *The Sphere*. Like in many cases where the site selected for the restaurant did not have adequate cooking facilities the food for this restaurant was prepared in a mobile van and transported to the restaurant.

The great popularity of the British Restaurants meant that word spread to areas which were not blessed with their own restaurants. The majority of the early restaurants were placed in towns and cities meaning that rural villages and hamlets missed out. In order to remedy this situation it was decided that emergency food vans which were not now needed as much in built up areas could provide a solution. From September 1941 to July 1942 these vans had sold nearly two million meals across nearly all parts of Britain. The vans picked up food which had been cooked at civic kitchens and drove a regular circular route stopping at pre-arranged points in villages and hamlets. The food was kept piping hot by the use of specially designed metal containers. Once more the press were keen to publicise this success which demonstrated that the supply of cheap and nutritious meals was something which everyone had access to. In July 1942, for example, *The Sphere* carried a short article highlighting this service in the Essex village of Stebbing which was part of a regular route for a van which sold meals that had been cooked at the British Restaurant in Dunmow.

Despite the popularity of the British Restaurants, however, the scheme fell flat in some areas. Local authorities were responsible for supplying the restaurants, although any losses were covered by the government, and some proved recalcitrant in funding them.

We have already seen how more isolated villages which had no British Restaurant of their own were being supplied by vans which carried meals cooked in nearby British Restaurants. Not every village and hamlet could be served, however. By 1943 this lack of service had been improved by the addition of a scheme which was the idea of the WI. This saw catering firms employed to send meat pies to isolated villages with each resident being entitled to one pie every week; the pies were distributed by local members of the WI.

By 1943 there were some 2,160 British Restaurants across the country and they were serving an estimated 600,000 meals per day. This was obviously a huge contribution not only to the war effort but also played a part in the increase in the general health of many British people.

In order to maintain this popularity it was essential that those who ran the restaurants were above board in their acquisition of food for the restaurants. In July 1943, however, the Southgate area of North London received something of a knock in confidence when it was discovered that horse meat had been used in a meat roll which had been supplied at the Palmadium British Restaurant. Further investigation had revealed that the local catering officer, Mr Hill, had failed to keep records of the purchasing of food for the British Restaurants in his charge. As a result, Mr Hill was immediately removed from his position, a new new catering officer, a Miss Rolfe, was appointed and all of the canteens and restaurants in the borough were to be reorganised.

Melksham's British Restaurant opened on 18 August 1943 in what was described as a 'pleasant, commodious building' which was sited at the Recreation Ground in the town. The main hall could hold 250 diners, had many windows, a spacious kitchen and was heated by a number of stoves. The building was dual purpose and it was envisaged that it might also be used to hold dances and so on. The main hall had approximately 60 tables each of which could seat four people.

Introducing Mrs Swanborough, who was to open the restaurant, Mr Hurn expressed the hope that it would be popular and well-used and profitable (despite the fact that British Restaurants were meant to be run on a not-for-profit basis) because if it did not attract customers it would be closed. More positively, Mrs Swanborough said that the British Restaurant had been planned and looked forward to for a long time in the town and urged people to make suggestions as to how improvements could be made before praising the Urban Council for its role in establishing the restaurant. Mrs Swanborough revealed that the menu for the first official day of opening the next day was to be roast beef, potatoes and beans followed by apple tart with custard. She then declared the restaurant open by pouring the first cups of tea herself. Although a large crowd attended the opening ceremony it seems that the council responsible might perhaps have had other things on their minds as both the chair and vice-chair were unable to attend and sent their apologies.

The British Restaurants were adaptable and were able to alter their menus according to what was available. They also adapted to their customer base with many, for example, in mining areas offering food which miners could take to work with them to eat during breaks in their shifts. The Chopwell British Restaurant in County Durham, for example, advertised meat pies, sausage rolls or Spam sandwiches at 4d, bacon or ham sandwiches for a penny more and teacakes with butter and jam for 3d.

By this stage the life of the village housewife had changed beyond recognition due to a variety of wartime necessities. The wives of agricultural labourers, for example, were already used to lives of hard work but transport continued to be a problem. For many, the nearest centre for shopping for essentials was several miles away and because of limited transport many women had to walk this distance. Added to their difficulties was rationing, the probability of their husband serving in the Home Guard, the possibility of having to billet land girls in their home and fire-watching duties. Despite these problems the women of agricultural workers continued to make huge voluntary contributions to the war effort through jam-making, gathering herbs and fruit, growing their own vegetables, raising pigs or hens and salvaging. In many villages the local WI organised jam-making classes and sessions. The jam had to conform to government regulations and was inspected but could also be sold.

The WVS volunteers who were largely responsible for operating the majority of British Restaurants and emergency feeding centres even had preparations well in hand for any dislocation caused by the D-Day invasion. In the belief that some thousands might be evacuated from locations close to the invasion ports the women of 8 Group (London) oversaw a highly successful exercise in which a semi-mobile cooking unit successfully prepared three-course meals for 400 diners at West Wickham (the unit was capable of providing food for a further 100 diners). The food, once cooked, was transported in metal containers to a British Restaurant some half a mile away where it was served up.

As what would prove to be the final year of the war opened, the Allies were advancing against Germany and many believed that 1945 would see the end of the war in Europe. For some local authorities concerns were already turning towards the financial viability of some wartime endeavours. Foremost amongst these concerns was the fate of various British Restaurants. Although the MoF was anxious that the scheme be continued it was the belief amongst some councils that the previous not-for-profit running of the restaurants would come to a quick end with the end of the conflict and that the government might prove reluctant to fund the restaurants, instead shifting this burden onto the local authorities.

At Driffield a meeting was held on 8 January at which the future of the town's British Restaurant was discussed. Councillor Hope posed the question of whether the restaurant was likely to become a charge on the rates while Councillor Redman stated that the restaurant had, for the first, time made a loss (although only of £1). This, he said, had been largely due to the schoolchildren who formed so much of the customer base had been off. Councillor Redman, however, said that he hoped that the restaurant could be kept open although the upper room might be rented out if the restaurant was to close.

The clerk put the accounts before the meeting and said that the balance in hand had been falling and that receipts had decreased considerably from £33 to £25 per week. Councillor Smith argued that rather than just looking at the monetary situation they should consider the good work that the restaurant had undertaken by feeding many schoolchildren and that if it had not been for the restaurant a great many children in the town would not have been provided with hot dinners.

The chairman, however, stated that he had just returned from the nearby town of Beverley where he had given notice that the British Restaurant there was to close. He had already asked the Education Committee to be ready to take it over as if the restaurant was not available to feed schoolchildren they would have to go elsewhere.

Councillor Redman, who had earlier appeared to be in two minds, then interjected. He said that arrangements to feed schoolchildren would have to be taken in hand by the Education Authority. Furthermore, he argued, that if the schoolchildren were taken away from the British Restaurant then the restaurant would never pay. Returns were diminishing now and 'he did not want to be on a sinking ship'.[5] The decision of the committee was to close the restaurant.

Other councils found themselves under pressure to close British Restaurants from the property owners. Many of the restaurants were housed in properties which had, up until the war, been used for other purposes and former owners in many cases wanted their properties returned to them without delay. In Eastbourne, for example, the owners of the Links guest house had allowed their property on Meads Road to be used as a British Restaurant but by February 1945 they were pressuring the council to return the property as they were keen to re-open for the forthcoming holiday season.

A meeting was therefore held on 26 February to discuss the matter of the Meads Road British Restaurant. At the meeting a message from the Wartime Meals Officer of the MoF was read out in which the official stated that the giving-up of emergency feeding centres was currently under consideration by the Ministry and the local authorities could expect guidance in the near future. After hearing this the committee decided to agree to close the British Restaurant on 31 March and the property be returned to its owners.

In some cases where substantial losses had been experienced the local authorities were even urged by the MoF to consider closures.

At Biggleswade, Bedfordshire, the MoF wrote to the Urban District Council in mid-April 1945 advising the council that it would be prudent to close the local British Restaurant. The council therefore voted to close the restaurant on 28 April. Work was taking place on a nearby housing development and one councillor moved an amendment that the closure of the restaurant be delayed for six weeks in order to allow the workmen to obtain meals at the restaurant. This was defeated after the committee was told that the men were to be housed in huts in nearby Sutton.

Even following the euphoria of VE-Day the MoF continued to warn of the possibility of severe food shortages in the winter of 1945/46 and local authorities were urged to keep British Restaurants open along with maintaining other wartime food production campaigns such as allotments and so on. Many local authorities were keen and even eager to do so but for others the monetary factor seems to have been the all-important consideration. As we have seen the MoF even urged closure in some cases.

In the suburban town of Kingswood to the east of Bristol the Urban District Council held its regular monthly meeting at the end of June. One of the main topics discussed was the fate of the town's British Restaurant. A letter had been received from the MoF urging the council to immediately close the restaurant. The council's chief financial officer presented the accounts to the committee. They showed that the restaurant had made a profit of £1 in May 1945 but that this was against depreciation of £9. This would, he argued, surely lead to administration. Explaining the MoF letter the clerk informed the committee that since its opening the restaurant had made a cash profit of £186 but depreciation amounted to £308 and the average number of meals served daily during May was only 81.

At Calne in Wiltshire a special meeting of the Town Council was held on the evening of 23 July at which the future of the town's British Restaurant was discussed. The British Restaurant Committee was proposing that the restaurant be immediately closed due to lack of trade. The committee reported that the trading accounts for the four-week period leading up to 28 May showed a trading loss of £40 and for the four week period up to 23 June a loss of £23. The Mayor supported the recommendation by saying that he saw no way in which the restaurant could be run without making a loss given the present turnover and operating expenses. The committee also informed the meeting that there had also been staffing problems over the previous two months and at the end of June it had looked like the restaurant would have to close immediately. This was averted but the restaurant was being run by just two people and a lunchtime volunteer. The committee expressed its deep regret over its recommendation, especially as the restaurant fed many children at lunchtime but argued that the responsibility for feeding these children lay with the local Education Authority. Moving the motion to close, the Mayor explained how in May an official from the MoF had visited and, despite the severe loss, had urged the committee to keep the restaurant open for a further three months with a smaller staff but that he could now not see how a profit could be made or how turnover could be increased.

The decision was supported by Alderman Gale. He believed the committee had come to a wise decision and he had personally thought that the British Restaurant had been redundant for some months.

Several councillors made vigorous objections to the attitude of the Mayor and the committee. Councillor F. Smith said that in light of the warning from the Minister of Food of upcoming shortages he believed it would be very wrong to close the restaurant. The attitude of the committee, he argued, was even more baffling as the MoF had agreed to cover the losses. Indeed, he concluded, the town had already seen shortages of food, especially meat, in the last three weeks which had in fact been worse than at any time during the war.

Supporting Councillor Smith, Councillor C. Ede (a doctor) argued that the restaurant was still providing some 124 dinners a day, half of those being to schoolchildren. After being interrupted by Alderman Gale, Dr Ede then moved that the MoF be informed of the exact position of the restaurant and asked for information and guidance as to whether the council could be assured of the necessary labour to staff the restaurant if it was to carry on. In this he was supported by several of his colleagues, including the Deputy Mayor.

Opposing Dr Ede's motion, Alderman Angell argued that the council should not involve the government in what was the small matter of a loss of £8-10 per week. Clearly there was a fear that the MoF, if involved, would order or at least urge the council to keep the restaurant open. At the end of the meeting, however, Dr Ede's motion was carried by eight votes to four.

Aftermath

Even after the end of the war with VJ-Day it was clear to many that rationing would continue for some time. Many ordinary Britons hoped, however, that this would be a period of months. They were to be sadly disappointed as the food supply situation was more dire than most imagined (although nowhere near as bad as it was in many parts of the world where starvation was a serious and tragic problem). Indeed, in the same month that victory was secured over Germany the bacon ration was cut from 4 oz to 3 oz, cooking fats from 2 oz to 1 oz, and part of the weekly meat allowance (reduced to 1s 6d at this point of the war) had to be taken in corned beef.

As a result of these problems, the Labour government which had swept to power in 1945 and which gave the British people such gifts as the National Health Service found itself unable to end rationing and had instead to enforce an austere policy. In 1946 a further blow fell when much of the harvest was ruined by heavy rain and, as a result, rationing was extended to bread (rationing was removed in 1948). Weather again intervened the next year when heavy snow and a long and deep frost destroyed many potato stores, necessitating the rationing of that staple too.

This continued austerity led to a great deal of anger and irritation amongst the British public who, having been victorious in the war, and having made very many sacrifices, could not understand why they were still in a worse position than they had been in 1939.

With the Conservatives and Winston Churchill having been removed from power in the General Election of 1945 many had hoped (rather naively) that rationing would soon end and things would return to some semblance of normality. The unpopular post-war rationing allowed Churchill to partially fight the 1950 General Election on the theme of handing back liberty to the British people in the form of ending rationing as soon as was possible. This policy had a widespread appeal, especially to many housewives who were frustrated by the continuance of rationing and Churchill and the Conservatives were victorious. Even so, many aspects of wartime food production and consumption remained in Britain for many years.

With the Conservatives returned to government with a mandate to remove rationing the British public had high hopes. In 1950 fruit (tinned and dried), jellies, mincemeat, syrup, treacle and chocolate biscuits were removed from the rationed list. In the same year, sliced and wrapped bread was again sold at stores for the first time since the war. Two years later tea rationing ended. In February 1953 confectionary rationing was ended and this was followed in September of that year by sugar. Finally, meat and all other food rationing was finally ended in Britain on 4 July 1954. It was not, however, the end of the wartime feeding experiment.

The End of the British Restaurant

Although, as we have seen, many British Restaurants closed down in 1945 as it became clear that the end of the war was in sight, others continued. Rationing, after all continued into the 1950s and in many places there was still a need for cheap, nutritional, communal feeding centres. The Labour government which came to power in the 1945 General Election held a belief that the British Restaurant might be the way of guaranteeing nourishing meals for all and in permanently equalising food consumption across the class system. The scheme, however, officially ended in 1947. The then Minister of Food, John Strachey, believed that the restaurants could end the largely middle-class dominance of private enterprise in the catering industry which was to the expense of the working-class. He thus enacted the Civic Restaurants Act which saw some British Restaurants become civic restaurants which were overseen by the local council. By 1949 there were still almost 700 such restaurants and, although the act allowed for the closure of civic restaurants if they failed to make a profit for three consecutive years, many persisted doggedly. Many soldiered on into the late 1960s and 1970s. Some new civic restaurants even opened in the 1970s. On 4 January 1972, for example, Coventry's council opened a civic restaurant in the form of an 88-seat licensed grill on Hertford Street.

A Final Example: The Highway Civic Restaurant, Gateshead

The civic restaurants became an increasingly politicised cause with Labour favouring them while the Conservative Party generally opposed them. One of the most determined hold-outs was the Highway Restaurant on Park Lane, Gateshead. For some years the restaurant had been making a loss but in March 1975 the council heard how numbers had increased the previous year. In November and December of 1973 the restaurant had sold only 600 meals but in a similar period in 1974 numbers had increased to between 1,800-2,400 alongside the serving of 300-1,200 meals served at civic functions. Despite this the restaurant was still showing a deficit of £2,160 and the Labour members still hoped that the fortunes of the restaurant could be turned around. This proved not to be the case, however, and losses of £3,000 in 1976 more than doubled in the next year to £7,000. Irate Conservative opposition members demanded the immediate closure of the restaurant but were resisted although the council leader admitted that the situation could not be allowed to grow worse.

The increasingly bitter political row over the Highway Restaurant continued with the Conservative Party leader on Gateshead Council writing to the auditor after it emerged in March 1978 that the council had borrowed money in order to pay for improvements to the restaurant after a health inspection highlighted 28 health risks.

Councillor John Hughes stated that he believed that the Public Protection Committee which oversaw the running of the restaurant had been misled over what the money was for. Councillor Hughes' Labour counterpart, Councillor Bill Collins, admitted that the committee had not been given the full story but claimed that this was so as not alarm the public and cause the restaurant further difficulties. The Tories claimed that this was deceitful and that the sum came to a loan of £4,000 plus £32 annual interest over the next five years.

Mid-May saw the attempt to immediately close the restaurant quashed in a private meeting of the council. By this point the Tories were claiming that ratepayers were funding the restaurant to the tune of £140 per week and that it was simply throwing money away. One Conservative, Councillor Bill Turnbull, claimed that the ongoing row over the restaurants £7,200 per year losses was 'the usual sorrowful saga of money down the drain'. The meeting at which the losses had been discussed had been closed to the press and public, but Councillor Turnbull told the press that this was 'the sort of thing people should hear about. This council is just throwing money away by keeping this restaurant open. It has been in the red for years now and is forecast to be in the red again next year.' He went on that the restaurant was serving no useful purpose and he did not see why ratepayers should fork out to keep it going. He admitted that the restaurant did provide a certain number of meals on wheels but claimed that 'these could be handled by school canteens', concluding that it was 'a scandalous waste of money'.

By 1978 the council was clearly aiming at keeping the Highway Restaurant going and adverts appeared throughout the year in which various offers were highlighted. In October, for example, prospective customers were told that from Monday-Friday they could enjoy the 50p Special. This was a choice of Cumberland sausage, steak and kidney pie, pasty, or pizza and a choice of chips, mashed potato, peas and bread and butter all for just 50p. Other offers included a one-third reduction on special lunches for senior citizens which ran from 1:30-3 pm. The three course a la carte menu was also still available.

By 1980, however, the OAP offer had been revealed as a flop as the offer only applied to the special three course lunches. By September of that year the council agreed to extend the offer to cover any meal.

The row continued to rumble on into the 1980s and by 1981 it was clear that the restaurant had become a political football between Labour and Conservative councillors in Gateshead. In January of that year a Conservative had made disparaging remarks in which he criticised the staff, service and quality of the meals being served. He also referred to the restaurant as a café. Unsurprisingly, the staff of the restaurant were angered by these allegations, and one wrote to the *Newcastle Journal* on 13 January repudiating the claims. The correspondent stated that all staff were fully trained and were appalled by the comments. The writer went on to say that they offered a valuable service for their regular customers, many of whom were senior citizens, as well as meals on wheels and luncheon clubs. Going on, the employee expressed how the staff objected to being used as political pawns and claimed that the Conservative group had visited the restaurant with the intention of finding things to criticise and their visit was an 'obvious, politically premeditated act, designed solely to be linked with their amendment to close' the restaurant in four months.[1]

Epilogue

No doubt many people were looking forward to the end of rationing with the end of the war but the more sober would have looked at the situation, heeded government warnings, and recognised that rationing would also be a part of post-war life for some considerable time after the victory celebrations had faded into memory.

In a sign of things to come, and in the immediate aftermath of VE-Day, the bacon ration was reduced from 4oz to 3oz and cooking fats from 2oz to 1oz. Furthermore, the public were told that part of their weekly meat allowance (reduced to 1s 6d at this point of the war) had to be taken in corned beef.

Britain had been left battered, both physically and financially, by the war and the election of a Labour government in 1945 had not found favour in the USA which withdrew much of its financial support in favour of rebuilding a strong post-war West Germany as a bulwark to oppose communism.

Another reason for the continuation of rationing was more humanitarian in nature. Millions of Europeans had been displaced during the war and many others faced the real possibility of dying of starvation. Even before VE-Day British forces had been trying to distribute food to the starving Dutch people who had still to be liberated. It was estimated that there were some three million Dutch people who were still under German control and in danger of starvation. Thus, on 29 April 1945, RAF Bomber Command launched Operation Manna which saw the heavy bombers of the force dropping food supplies to these desperate people.

The plight of the Dutch people gained most attention but there were also large numbers of people in other previously occupied countries such as Belgium and Denmark who were being forced to survive on what amounted to a starvation diet. Furthermore, many German people were also in danger of starvation after the war. The British government, therefore, took the courageous decision to divert supplies to these areas and to continue with rationing. This was despite the fact that there were now greater supplies of food, especially beef, lamb, butter and cheese, from overseas available to the country, especially from countries such as Australia, Canada and New Zealand. Ireland also began to provide greater quantities of dairy products and safe shipping lanes meant that quantities of beef (both frozen and tinned) could be imported from Argentina.

One result of America diverting more supplies to mainland Europe was that the wartime staple of Spam became a relatively sparse commodity and was largely replaced by imports of corned beef from South America (notably Argentine and Uruguay) with the most common variety being that of Fray Bentos.

The humanitarian nature of Britain's decision to go without in order to provide food to Europe was not without controversy. Critics claimed that the Attlee government was cynically using shortages in Britain as leverage in order to persuade the USA to take over the responsibility of feeding Germans in the British controlled zone of Germany and to hopefully gain access to funds from the Marshall Plan in order to rebuild wartime damage.

Indeed, bread, which had never been rationed during the war, was added to the rationed list on 21 July 1946 despite having seemingly secured supplies of Canadian wheat through the signature of a four-year contract with that country just three days after the bread ration was introduced.

The rationing on bread was not to end until 25 July 1948 but even then the only bread that was available to the public was the unpopular National Loaf and it was not until 1950 that the British public was to be able to purchase sliced and wrapped bread. In the event the National Loaf was not completely abandoned until 1956, when people overwhelmingly returned to white bread.

Potatoes were also added to the rationed list in 1947 and the majority of rationed items continued to be controlled throughout the 1940s (although clothes rationing was abolished in 1949). After this there were some improvements with rationing ending for several sweet items including chocolate biscuits, tinned fruit and syrup in May 1950. In October 1952, to the relief on many, tea rationing was ended and the children of Britain were no doubt delighted when sweet rationing ended in February of the following year.

At the time of the coronation of Queen Elizabeth II in June 1953, however, there were still important items on the rationed list including sugar (which was not taken off ration until September), butter and cheese.

Rationing was eventually ended on 4 July 1954 when the wartime measure had lasted some fourteen years since its introduction. Overall, the policy had been a success and, while it enjoyed mixed popularity, had been of great benefit to the war effort. There had also been unforeseen benefits. One of these was a general improvement in the dietary health of the population. In general, people consumed less eggs, fat, meat, and sugar due to rationing and shortages. There was actually a reduction in the frequency of deaths from heart attacks and strokes during the war. Some scientists claimed that this was a direct result of the more healthy diet imposed by rationing. The poorest sections of society (along with children, the elderly and pregnant women) actually gained the most due to rationing as their previously poor diet was supplemented and their intakes of proteins and vitamins actually increased thanks to rationing. In general it can be said that the rationing system of the Second World War and the willingness of the British people, in general, to embrace it and to grow their own food proved to be a massive success and, perhaps, provides very valuable clues as to how future food shortages could be avoided.

Appendix I

Recipes

PEMBROKESHIRE PUDDING (4 SERVINGS)

Ingredients
½ lb sausage meat
½ onion, finely chopped
1½ lb boiled potatoes
1-2 tbsp of milk
2 tbsp grated cheese
Salt and pepper

Method
Skin the sausages and mix with the finely chopped onion. Mash the boiled potatoes with the milk and season with salt and pepper. Spread a layer of potato in the bottom of a pie dish and on this place a layer of the sausage and onion. Top with another layer of potato and sprinkle with grated cheese. Bake in the oven until nicely browned.

CABBAGE AND SAUSAGE SCRAMBLE (4 SERVINGS)

Ingredients
1½ lb shredded cabbage
½ lb potato (thinly sliced)
2 oz chopped leek
½ lb sausage meat
1½ oz cooking fat

½ pint of water
1 tsp meat extract
Salt and pepper

Method

Heat the fat in a frying pan. Add the cabbage, potato and leek. Cook gently for ten minutes, turning frequently, but do not brown. Add the sausage meat, broken up into small pieces, seasoning and meat extract dissolved in water. Cover the pan and simmer for 20-35 minutes. Stir occasionally to prevent sticking.

MEAT ROLL (4 SERVINGS)

Ingredients

½ lb sausage meat
½ teacup oatmeal
½ beef cube
¼ pint of water
½ small leek or 1 onion, chopped
1 reconstituted dried egg
Salt and pepper
Pinch of mixed herbs

Method

Mix sausage meat and oatmeal, and beef cube dissolved in boiling water. Add the leek or onion and the seasoning. To allow the oatmeal to swell a little more water may be needed. The mixture should be fairly soft. Grease a small mould or teacup, pour in the reconstituted egg. Stand in a saucepan with a little boiling water, cover with greased paper and steam for about 15 minutes. Allow to cool. Place a layer of the sausage meat mixture in the greased mould. Add the eggs cut in slices, then the remainder of the sausage mixture. Steam for 1½ hours. Turn out when cold.

SAVOURY BREAD PUDDING

Ingredients
½ pint thin white sauce
1 egg
¾ lbs cooked vegetables
6 oz breadcrumbs
parsley
salt and pepper

Method
Put thick layer of vegetables in a pie dish and cover with breadcrumbs. Mix a good dessertspoonful of chopped parsley with the salt and pepper in the vegetable liquid. Thicken with a little cornflour mixed with milk to make the white sauce. Stir beaten egg into the sauce and pour over contents of pie dish. Bake in moderate oven until set (approx. 15 mins).

SAVOURY RISSOLES

Ingredients
1½ lbs of cooked mixed vegetables
4 tbsp dried egg
4 oz breadcrumbs
4 tbsp chopped parsley
salt and pepper
browned breadcrumbs
2/3 tbsp dripping

Method
Mix the vegetables, crumbs, parsley and dried egg. Season with pepper and salt. Form into rissoles and roll in the browned crumbs. Melt the fat in a frying pan or baking tin and fry or bake the rissoles until brown all over.

BEEF RISSOLES

Ingredients
beef leftovers
equal quantity of breadcrumbs
salt and pepper
mixed herbs
leftover gravy

Method
Mince the beef and mix with the breadcrumbs. Season well with pepper and salt and add small quantity of mixed herbs. Moisten with gravy until mixture is a fairly stiff paste. Divide into small pieces and form into cakes. Fry in a deep frying pan half-full of hot dripping. Drain and bring to the table.

Excellent served with pickles.

SUET PASTRY

Ingredients
¼ lb flour
¼ lb mashed potato or oatmeal
2 oz suet
1 tsp baking powder
¼ tsp salt
cold water

Method
Mix all the ingredients and add water to form an elastic dough. Bake as for ordinary pastry.

CHICKEN OR RABBIT PIE

Ingredients
1 rabbit
1 reconstituted egg, scrambled
1 tsp finely chopped parsley
1tbsp chopped white celery
2 slices of bacon
½ pint of rabbit stock
2-3 leaves of gelatine
salt and pepper

Method
For the pastry
6 oz flour
3 oz lard
pinch of salt
cold water

Make the stocks from the head flaps and helmet of rabbit. Mix celery and parsley with salt and pepper. Remove rind from bacon and cut into small pieces. Cut scrambled egg into walnut sized pieces.

Joint the rabbit and toss pieces in the parsley mix. Pack into a pie dish leaving a hole in the middle, layering on the egg and bacon. Put in enough stock to create steam, but not enough to boil over.

For the pastry – Sieve flour and salt. Cut in lard and mix with enough water to form a paste. Roll out until an inch bigger than pie dish. Cut strip approximately ¾ inch wide and place around rim of dish, brush with water or reconstituted egg. Place pastry on top of pie and press together and flute at edges. Glaze with egg and make cut in centre. Place in hot oven until pastry is cooked then reduce heat until rabbit is cooked and tender. Melt gelatine in remaining stock and pour through hole in centre. Rock dish to spread gelatine stock and leave for one day. Serve cold with salad.

CARROT MARMALADE

Ingredients
2 lbs carrots, washed, scraped and grated
1½ lbs sugar (warmed)
equivalent lemon substitute for 2 lemons

Method
Place the carrots in a preserving pan with just enough boiling water to prevent the pan from burning. Cook until tender, adding a little more water if necessary. Add the sugar and lemon substitute. Bring back to the boil and cook until a chutney consistency is reached (about 45 minutes).

A really pleasing substitute for the orange marmalade you can't make! (but it will not keep, so do not make any more than two weeks supply).

MOCK GOOSE

Ingredients
1 lb sheep's liver
6 oz fat pork
1½ lbs potatoes
2 leeks
1 tbsp flour
2 tsp powdered sage
salt and pepper
dripping
¼ pint stock or water
1 chopped apple

Method
Grease a pie dish. Cut the pork into dice and wash, dry and slice the liver thinly. Mix the sage with the flour and seasoning and dip the

liver and pork into this. Slice the potatoes and leeks thinly. Arrange the meat in the pie dish in alternate layers with the potatoes, apple and leeks. Add the stock or water and cover with a good layer of potato. Put some small pieces of dripping on top and cover all with greased paper. Bake in a moderate oven for 1½ hours. About 15 minutes before serving remove the paper and allow the potatoes to brown.

MOCK CRAB ON TOAST

Ingredients
2 oz grated cheese
¼ tsp mustard
1 tsp anchovy essence
1 tsp vinegar
3 tbsp white sauce
½ oz melted margarine
hot margarine toast
1 tsp finely chopped parsley
pinch of pepper

Method
Mix all the ingredients well together. Pile on pieces of hot toast and put into a hot oven, or under the gas grill, to heat thoroughly and slightly brown the top. Sprinkle with parsley and serve at once.

VEGETABLE HOT-POT

Ingredients
2oz leeks or onions
4 oz carrots
4 oz turnip
¾ lb potatoes

½ tsp mixed herbs
½ tsp salt and pepper to taste

Method
Dice carrot and turnip, slice onions and potatoes. Place carrots, turnip and onions in dish and cover with water before placing the sliced potatoes on top. Cook for two hours in a moderate oven with a lid on the dish. When peas are in season they can be used in place of one vegetable.

LEEK PUDDING

Ingredients
8 oz flour
1 oz fat
1 oz grated potato
2 level tsp baking powder
1 level tsp salt
8 oz finely chopped leek
Water to mix

Method
Mix together all ingredients and add enough water to create a stiff batter. Place into a greased basin and steam for 1-1½ hours. Serve with gravy or cheese sauce.

SPRING VICTORY

Ingredients
4 level tsp dried egg
1 carrot
1 turnip

2 oz swede
2 oz cabbage
2 spring onions
For the White Sauce:
2 oz margarine
2 oz flour
½ oz milk powder
¼ pint water

Method

Dice and cook vegetables in salted water before draining well. Make the sauce, add vegetables and half the reconstituted egg, mix well and turn onto a tray to cool. Mould into shapes, roll in flour or breadcrumbs and fry until golden brown. Scramble the remaining egg and pile into the middle of the dish before arranging the croquettes around.

CORNED BEEF PIE

Ingredients

3 rations of corned beef (6d worth)
1 cup finely shredded raw vegetables
1 dsp flour
1 Oxo cube
A small piece of fat
Shortcrust pastry (made with 6 oz flour and 3 oz fat)
1 tsp chopped parsley

Method

Melt fat in small frying pan and fry the vegetables lightly before stirring in the flour and cooking for a few minutes. Add one cup of cold water into which the Oxo cube has been crumbled and stir until thickened. Take off the heat and add cubed corned beef, parsley and salt and pepper to taste. Line a small plate with pastry and spread on the meat mixture before covering with pastry, crimping edges and decorating with small pastry leaves. Bake in a moderate oven for half and hour.

CORNED BEEF TURNOVER

Ingredients
8 oz corned beef
1½ lb potatoes
Small piece of fat
Small onion
Oxo cube

Method
Dissolve the Oxo cube in a small cup of hot water, peel the potatoes and cut them into ½ inch dice. Then dice the meat, mince the onion and mix with the potatoes before seasoning and moistening with the Oxo cube. Melt the fat in a heavy based frying pan until smoking hot and then add the meat and vegetable mixture, flattening it down to form a flat cake. Cover and reduce the heat to a gentle heat and cook for approximately 40 minutes (the potatoes should be cooked and the underside crisp and browned). Fold over and place on a warmed serving plate, garnish with parsley.

SPICE PIE

Ingredients
1 lb finely grated carrots
2 dessertspoons of sugar
½ tsp mixed spice
1 heaped dessertspoon cornflour
1 lb short or potato pastry

Method

Place grated carrot into a saucepan with the sugar and spice, and the cornflour previously mixed with ½ pint of water. Stir until the mixture thickens. Have ready a tart tin lined with crust, the edge well pressed and up and fluted. Pour in the mixture and bake in a moderate oven until the crust is a golden brown all around the edge. Dust with nutmeg (if liked) and serve cold (serves 4).

Appendix II

A Brief Timeline of Rationing

1940

8 January: the first foods rationed were butter (4oz), sugar (12oz) and ham or bacon (4oz), per person per week.

11 March: Meat in general was added to the ration list. 1s 10d per person at first. The MoF estimated that this would allow for an average of approximately 1lb of meat a week per person.

July: tea, 2oz tea per person, per week.

1941

March: Jam, marmalade, syrup, and treacle added to list (8oz per month).

5 May: Cheese. 1oz per person per week, increased a month later to 2oz per person per week.

July: sugar ration was doubled for summer months to encourage people to make their own fruit preserves and jams.

November: Controls introduced on milk, canned meats, fish and some vegetables.

1942

January: Rice and dried fruit rationed.

9 February: Condensed milk, breakfast cereals, tinned tomatoes, tinned peas, and soap.

26 July: Sweets and chocolate added to ration list.

August: Biscuits rationed.

December: Oats added to ration list.

1943
Sausages added to rationed list.

June: Individual jam ration could be taken in sugar instead.

1945
27 May: Bacon ration cut from 4oz to 3oz, cooking fats from 2oz to 1oz, and part of the weekly meat allowance (reduced to 1s 6d at this point of the war) had to be taken in corned beef.

1946
Bread rationing introduced.

1947
Potato rationing introduced.

1948
25 July: Flour and bread rationing ends.

1949
15 March: Clothing rationing ends.

1950
19 May: Rationing ends for fruit (tinned and dried), jellies, mincemeat, syrup, treacle and chocolate biscuits.

Sliced, wrapped bread allowed again at stores.

1952
3 October: Tea rationing ends.

1953

5 February: Sweet rationing ends.

September: Sugar rationing ends.

1954

4 July: All remaining rationing is abolished.

Endnotes

Chapter 1

1. Alan F. Wilt, *Food for War: Agriculture and Rearmament in Britain Before the Second World War* (Oxford University Press, 2001), p. 188.
2. Calder, A., *The People's War: Britain 1939-1945* (Pimlico, 1992), pp. 423–4.
3. *Berwick Advertiser*, 10 April 1941, p. 5.
4. *Staffordshire Advertiser*, 9 September 1939, p. 2.
5. Interview, NS/RA2, 2001.
6. Calder, A., *The People's War*, p 416.
7. Interview, NS/RA1, 2001.
8. Calder, A., *The People's War*, pp 415-416.
9. Longmate, N., *How We Lived Then: A History of Everyday Life During the Second World War* (Arrow, 1973), pp 142-143–3.
10. Tyne & Wear Archives Service (TWAS): G/TFB/1/1. Tyne Fishery Board: annual reports and yearbooks, 1939—1944, p 15.
11. *Ibid*, p 14.
12. *Ibid*, pp 14-—15.
13. *Ibid*, pp 20–21.

Chapter 2

1. *The Scotsman*, 8 January 1943, p. 3.

Chapter 3

1. Zweiniger-Bargielowska, I., *Austerity in Britain. Rationing, Controls, and Consumption 1939-1955* (Oxford University Press, 2002), p 13.
2. The debate over what type of meal was which echoed the debate over Scotch Eggs during the recovery from the Covid crisis in Britain.
3. *Sunderland Daily Echo & Shipping Gazette,* 6 September 1939, p. 3.
4. Zweiniger-Bargielowska, I., *Austerity*, p 60.
5. Anderson, C. A., 'Food Rationing and Morale', *American Sociological Review*, 8, 1 (Feb. 1943), p 24.
6. TWAS: PA/NC/5/55. Summary of Reports, Newcastle upon Tyne, 15 July 1941.
7. *Ibid*, 25 April 1940.
8. *Ibid*, 27 September 1940.
9. *Ibid*, 25 October 1940.
10. *Ibid*, 4 January–1 March 1941.
11. Longmate, N, *How We Lived Then*, pp 144–5.
12. TWAS: TU/BA/1/1. Newcastle, Gateshead and District Butchers' Association, minutes, 27 May 1940, p 399.
13. *Morpeth Herald*, 5 December 1941, p. 4.
14. Longmate, N., *How We Lived Then*, p 145.
15. Titmuss, R M., *Problems of Social Policy* (HMSO, 1950), p 513.
16. Zweiniger-Bargielowska, I., *Austerity*, p 139.
17. TWAS: PA/NC/5/55. Summary of reports, Newcastle upon Tyne, 27 March 1942.
18. Ministry of Food memorandum, 30 April 1942, in ibid.
19. TWAS: PA/NC/5/55, 19 September 19th 1944.
20. TWAS: PA/NC/5/55. Summary of reports, Newcastle upon Tyne, 14 March 14th 1941, and 12 September 12th 1941.

21. TWAS: TU/BA/1/1. Newcastle, Gateshead and District Butchers' Association, minute book, special committee, 11 September 11th 1939, pp 371–2-372.

22. *Ibid*, 27 May 1940, p 399.

23. *Ibid*, 6 November 1940, p 412.

24. TWAS: MD/NC/5/55. Summary of Reports, Newcastle City Police, 4 January 4th 1941.

25. *Edinburgh Evening News*, 22 July 1942, p. 4.

26. Correspondence from Mrs M. Playle, 2001.

27. Vicomte de Mauduit had been educated in England and was a trained engineer who had been badly injured during the First World War while serving with the French Air Force. Following the publication of his book, he vanished from sight and it was later revealed that he had been found guilty of making statements likely to cause alarm or despondency and sentenced to two months' imprisonment. Following this treatment, he had relocated to France and became a critic of both Britain and the Free-French government. In an article published in 1942-1943 he criticised his treatment in Britain and alleged that French volunteers who arrived in Britain were poorly treated. He made similar criticisms in a radio broadcast on Radio-Paris in January 1943. After 1943, he once again disappeared from sight and it was not until after the war that his fate was revealed. He had been recorded as arriving at Dachau Concentration Camp in June 1944 and his death there occurred on 2 February 1945.

28. Anonymous correspondence, 2001.

29. *Morpeth Herald*, 5 September 1941, p. 2.

30. *Dundee Evening Telegraph*, 8 August 1941, p. 5.

31. *The Scotsman*, 9 August 1941, p. 3.

32. *The Scotsman*, 22 October 1941, p. 3.

33. *The Scotsman*, 19 December 1941, p. 6.

34. *The Scotsman*, 19 December 1941, p. 6.

Chapter 4

1. Alnwick & County County Gazette & Guardian, 1st September 1939, p. 3.
2. *Orkney Herald*, 21 August 1940, p. 6.
3. *Sunderland Echo and Shipping Gazette*, 31 January 1940, p.5.
4. *Daily Mirror*, 21 January 1943, p. 5.
5. The song was written by Betty Driver. She later went on to portray the long-running character of Betty Williams in Coronation Street. The character, interestingly, was known for her Lancashire hotpot, using potatoes.
6. Zweiniger-Bargielowska, I., *Austerity*, p. 66.
7. TWAS: PA/NC/5/55. Summary of Reports, Newcastle upon Tyne, 29 March 1941.
8. Correspondence from Mrs M. Playle, 2001.
9. North Shields Library website [http://www.libraryclub.co.uk/Memories/memory_1.html], April 2004.
10. TWAS: PA/NC/5/55. Summary of Reports, Newcastle upon Tyne, 16 January 1942.
11. TWAS: PA/NC/5/55. Summary of Reports, Newcastle upon Tyne, 4 January 1941.
12. TWAS: PA/NC/5/55. Summary of Reports, Newcastle upon Tyne, 16 January 1942.

Chapter 5

1. *The Bystander*, 16 October 1940, p. 34.
2. *Daily Mirror*, 25 August 1941, p. 3.
3. Barbara Mullen had first appeared on the London stage in the theatre version of *Jeannie* in 1938. She went on to appear in roles such as Mrs De Winter in *Rebecca*, Maggie in *What Every Woman Knows* and Miss Marple in *The Murder at the Vicarage*.

She appeared in more than 20 films and in numerous TV shows. In later life she found even greater fame with her portrayal of Janet McPherson, the efficient housekeeper, in *Dr Finlay's Casebook.*
4. *Daily Herald*, 10 November 1941, p. 3.
5. *Driffield Times*, 13 January 1945, p. 4.

Aftermath

1. Newcastle Journal, 13 January 1981, p.7.

Index